ADOLESCENCE

Adolescence is one of a series of low-cost books under the title PSYCHOANALYTIC **ideas** which brings together the best of Public Lectures and other writings given by analysts of the British Psycho-Analytical Society on important psychoanalytic subjects.

The books can be ordered from:
Karnac Books
www.karnacbooks.com
Tel. +(0)20 8969 4454
Fax: +(0)20 8969 5585
E-mail: shop@karnacbooks.com

Other titles in the Psychoanalytic ideas Series:

Shame and Jealousy: The Hidden Turmoils
Phil Mollon

Dreaming and Thinking
Rosine Jozef Perelberg

Spilt Milk: Perinatal Loss and Breakdown
Joan Raphael-Leff (editor)

Unconscious Phantasy
Riccardo Steiner (editor)

Psychosis (Madness)
Paul Williams (editor)

ADOLESCENCE

Editor

Inge Wise

Series Editors

Inge Wise and *Paul Williams*

KARNAC

LONDON   NEW YORK

First published in 2000 by the Institute of Psycho-Analysis, London

Reprinted in 2004 by
H. Karnac (Books) Ltd.
6 Pembroke Buildings, London NW10 6RE

British Library Cataloguing in Publication Data

A C.I.P. for this book is available from the British Library

  ISBN 1 85575 380 4

Designed typeset and produced by The Studio Publishing Services Ltd,
Exeter EX4 8JN

Printed in Great Britain

10 9 8 7 6 5 4 3 2 1

www.karnacbooks.com

CONTENTS

CHAPTER FOUR
Adolescence   67
  Denis Flynn

CHAPTER FIVE
Working with addicts   87
  Luis Rodríguez de la Sierra

ACKNOWLEDGEMENTS

I wish to thank all those whose ideas and efforts have continued to contribute to *Psychoanalytic ideas*: Susan Budd, Dr Anthony Bateman and all other members of the Publication Committee, the reviewers for the critical and thoughtful analysis of the individual lectures, L. Moncada for her comments, Linda Carter-Jackson and Nick Hall at the Institute of Psycho-Analysis, Lyndsay MacDonald for administrative expertise, Dr Martin Edwards for copy-editing, Phil Baines for his design and enthusiasm, Judith Perle for editorial help and Professor Dr Paul Williams for much hard work and moral support.

Inge Wise
Series Editor

Dr Abrahão H Brafman, Member of the British Psycho-Analytical Society, qualified in adult and child psychoanalysis. He was a Consultant Child and Adolescent Psychiatrist in the NHS and a Consultant at the London Clinic of Psycho-Analysis, and is now a Consultant for the British Association of Psychotherapists and Honorary Senior Lecturer at the Psychotherapy Department of University College Hospital, London. His particular interests are child development and the mutual influences between children and parents.

Dr Catalina Bronstein, Training Analyst of the British Psycho-Analytical Society, qualified as a psychiatrist in Buenos Aires. She trained as a child psychotherapist at the Tavistock Clinic and now works at the Brent Adolescent Centre and in private practice with adults and adolescents. She is Honorary Senior Lecturer at University College London, writes and lectures on the psychoanalytic understanding of adolescents' problems, and teaches at the Tavistock and abroad.

Donald Campbell, Training Analyst, former President of the British Psycho-Analytical Society, also trained as a Child and Adolescent Analyst at the Anna Freud Clinic. He is a Consultant Child Psychotherapist and a past chairman of the Portman Clinic, and has published on violence, suicide, child sex abuse and adolescence.

Denis Flynn, Member of the British Psycho-Analytical Society, is Head of the Inpatient Adolescent Unit at the Cassel Hospital and works in private psychoanalytic practice. He trained at the Tavistock Clinic as a child and adolescent psychotherapist, and has degrees in Philosophy and Social Sciences.

Dr Luis Rodríguez de la Sierra is a Training Analyst and Child Analyst of the British Psycho-Analytical Society, and works at the Department of Psychotherapy at University College London, the Anna Freud Clinic, the London Clinic of Psycho-Analysis and in private practice. He has published papers on child analysis and drug addiction.

Inge Wise, Member of the British Psycho-Analytical Society, trained in marital and adult psychotherapy at the Tavistock Clinic. She is a Consultant to a research project on adolescent identity in post-Communist countries, and works in private practice, lectures and teaches in this country and abroad.

Introduction

Inge Wise

Adolescence—when we are no longer children and have not yet reached adulthood—is a time of much disturbance, change and potential for growth. The adolescent is confronted with a body that stretches, changes and grows in all directions, as does her or his mind: he is no longer who he was.

Unresolved conflicts pertaining to infancy and childhood need to be worked through once more by the adolescent, who is struggling to find an identity of his own. Oedipal longings and desires come to the fore a second time round in the (unconscious) hope of finding a better solution as the adolescent increasingly turns away from parents and family towards friends and peers—beyond the familiar world of parents and school.

Whilst this is a time of turbulence, disturbance and struggle, often of inner uncertainties and chaos, the adolescent's growing discovery of his own sexually maturing body and physical strength, alongside his developing mind and intellect, usually enables him to move from dependence towards independence.

Thus adolescence—a developmental and maturational stage— makes great demands on the adolescent, who is called upon by parents and society at large to get on with the task of sorting out the enormous upheaval in his inner world. As this process becomes established and new solutions are found to old inner conflicts, the adolescent's powerful energies turn towards reality testing and the turmoil and conflicting demands of his inner and outer worlds. Creativity, love and hope battle with hatred, aggression, violence, depression and suicidal despair.

All this takes time. The age from 12/13 to 20 years used to be defined as adolescence. It seems to take longer now; 12 to 25 years of age (or even later) is a not uncommon time span in today's uncertain and complex times. Normal adolescent development includes unpredictable and sudden changes in the adolescent's mind, as he is confronted from the onset of puberty with inner turmoil, his emerging adolescent/adult sexuality and the constraints of his conscience. By contrast, fixed or inflexible feelings and behaviour are signs of psychopathology, requiring treatment. When breakdown of any kind occurs, the troubled adolescent in need of help is often brought for treatment by his parents, although the existence of Walk-In Clinics (a list of which appears in the Appendix) facilitates self-referral by the adolescent.

What sort of treatment is on offer and what is the treatment of choice? As M. Laufer (1995) says:

> . . . the issue should not be viewed as one form of treatment versus the other, but instead should be decided on the basis of which treatment can address itself to the psychopathology and can offer the adolescent the means of altering the direction of his development so that his sexual and social life by the end of adolescence and during his adult life will be determined by non-pathological factors rather than by the pathology which was the cause of his anxiety and for which he sought help in the first place.

Laufer goes on to say:

> It is most appropriate and most possible to enable a treatment process to develop with adolescents from the age of 16. The younger adolescent is still too absorbed in his efforts to begin to remove himself emotionally from the Oedipal parents, and the time up to about the age of 16 is one which is characterized by the adolescent still feeling that his body does not yet belong to him, but is still the property of the Oedipal parents, especially the mother.

Speaking of the aims of treatment, Laufer stresses the signifi-cance of working in the transference. This is vital for the under-standing and the undoing of psychopathology. In addition, because dealing with adolescents evokes strong counter-transference feel-ings in those working with them, it is of particular importance to the therapist to have institutional support in the form of case discussions/seminars.

All five authors whose Public Lectures on adolescence make up this book work, or have worked, in clinics or hospital departments specially organized along these lines.

These Public Lectures present five different perspectives on working with adolescents. D. Campbell examines the choice of violence as a defence against breakdown. C. Bronstein conceptual-izes suicidal tendencies. A. H. Brafman stresses the importance both of the relationship between patient and analyst, and of bearing in mind parental needs and emotional involvement. D. Flynn discusses in detail the ambivalence that adolescents feel in relation to their selves, their bodies and their Oedipal objects. L. Rodriguez de la Sierra reflects on the difficulties the analyst encounters in working with adolescent addicts.

In the chapter "Violence as a defence against breakdown in adolescence", Campbell examines the choice of a violent role model or ego ideal and its defensive functions, tracing its aetiology from Stan's early childhood to the age of 16, when Stan started weekly psychotherapy. The death of a younger brother and the birth of a physically disabled one added to his mother's depression; and preoccupation with his disabled sibling, his father's violent behav-iour and both parents' emotional unavailability left Stan vulnera-ble, bereft and isolated.

Campbell acknowledges that:

> It is not uncommon for an adolescent in search of a gender role identity to express his developing adult sexuality to identify with contemporary heroes (e.g. pop stars and sports heroes).

Stan identified with a violent and destructive android from the film *Blade Runner*: ". . . alive on the outside but only mechanical on the inside".

Suicidal thoughts appeared as Stan developed the capacity to think about and to understand his violent fantasies before acting on them. Such thoughts are not unusual in adolescence. They are not in themselves a sign of serious disturbance, although attempted suicide is. Bronstein's chapter, based on her work with suicidal adolescents, stresses the impact of the onrush of adolescent/adult sexuality at the onset of puberty, together with physical growth, on the adolescent's inner and outer worlds. The loss of childhood, the growing awareness of time passing, of their own and parental mortality, and overwhelming anxieties in relation to these collide with feelings of omnipotence and youthful exuberance.

Sally, Bronstein's patient, a 15-year-old girl who misses more sessions than she attends, does attempt suicide. She seems caught in a self-destructive, sado-masochistic cycle from which suicide is felt to offer the only way out. Bronstein remarks, talking about Sally, that:

> treating these adolescents, the analyst is usually left ... with the feeling that one has to wait, not knowing, whether they are going to kill themselves or not. but without giving up hope.

Brafman's chapter presents a schematic overview of issues involved in a psychoanalytic/psychotherapeutic approach to adolescents. It also reflects a Winnicottian perspective and the wisdom drawn from his experience of working over several decades with adolescents in a variety of settings. He particularly stresses the importance of offering treatment to the patient's parents in order to attend to their needs as well.

Flynn reminds us that "our psychoanalytical understanding of adolescence has only really moved forwards in the last 50 years." He links this to the time after the Second World War, when adolescence first became a phenomenon meriting research and investigation. He acknowledges the continuing validity of Sigmund Freud's developmental model contained in "Three essays on the theory of sexuality". His overview of relevant psychoanalytical literature includes M. Klein, A. Freud, W. Bion, R. Hinshelwood, D. Stern, R. Britton, M. & E. Laufer and H. Rosenfeld among others. I have included essential source works by some of these (and other) authors in my references. Flynn presents the case study of Fiona, a troubled girl, on the verge of puberty, who becomes able to acknowledge her ambivalent feelings about herself and her Oedipal objects during her treatment.

Rodriguez de la Sierra's chapter is based on his work with addicts. He locates the unconscious conflicts and the psychopathology of the addict as being:

> . . . not as early as those involved in psychosis, and not as late as the psychoneuroses . . . [with] three predominant aspects: depression, paranoia and perversion.

A detailed analysis of the psychopathology of addiction is linked to several tragic case histories. The self-destructive, sado-masochistic and persecutory nature of the objects in the addict's inner world makes these particularly slow and painful analyses, involving the modification of parameters and tolerance by the analyst of excessive demands and neediness. Quotes from J. Glover, H. Rosenfeld, J. Mannheim, A. Limentani, P. Greenacre and others are woven into the narrative, giving a comprehensive overview and helping us to glimpse the complex and dedicated work the analysis of adolescent addicts requires.

Reference and source texts

Blos, P. (1996). *On Adolescence. A Psychoanalytic Interpretation*, Free Press.

Erikson, E. (1965). *Childhood and Society*, Hogarth.

Freud, A. (1958). Adolescence in *Psychoanalytic Study of the Child*, 8, pp. 255–78.

Jones, E. (1922). Some problems of adolescence. Reprinted in *Collected Papers*, Maresfield, 1948.

Laufer, M. (1995). Problems of assessment and treatment in adolescence. Unpublished Public Lecture, London.

Winnicott, D. (1963). Hospital care supplementing psychotherapy in adolescence. Reprinted in *The Maturational Process and the Facilitating Environment*, Hogarth, 1965.

CHAPTER ONE

Violence as a defence against breakdown in adolescence

Donald Campbell

Introduction

The individual who is prone to violent behaviour as a means of resolving internal conflicts is influenced by a continuing, conscious or unconscious fantasy life that is dominated by violence.[1] In this chapter I will examine the choice and function of a violent role model or ego ideal before and after puberty and the part it plays in reinforcing violence as a defence against breakdown in adolescence. I will illustrate my points with case material from a 16-year-old adolescent I will call Stan, who physically attacked another boy. After being taunted by an intimidating bully named Grummond, Stan took his father's cricket bat and hit Grummond repeatedly. He was quickly restrained by a number of his friends, although he struggled to inflict more injury on Grummond.

A general view of Stan's violence

In this chapter I define violence in Nigel Walker's (1991) terms as the intended infliction of bodily harm. I have found it useful to distinguish between two types of violence as described by Glasser (1979), self-preservative and sadistic. The aim of a self-preservative act of violence is the negation of a threat to physical or psychological survival.[2] In speaking about psychological survival I am referring to that which we associate with our identity, with a stability of the self that we may experience as a state of well-being. Psychological survival is dependent on many different factors, such as self-esteem, safety, biological needs and good enough relationships, and is threatened when any of these components are at risk. Fonagy & Target (1995) have linked a reliance upon violence to a developmental failure to meet the fundamental need of every infant to find his own mind, his intentional state, in the mind of the object. When the child cannot find itself in the mind of its mother due to her depression or psychotic state, the child relies less on words to engage her mind and more upon actions directed at the mother's body in order to create a presence in her mind. Nowhere is this more evident than in the use of sadistic acts to dominate the victim's mind. In his treatment of individuals who perpetrated apparently random assaults, Sohn (1995) found that a series of losses, real or imagined, resulted in early failure to sublimate aggression and develop a language through which to project feelings. This, in turn, increased his patients' expression of violent muscularity.

Sadistic violence differs from self-preservative violence in that it aims to make the victim suffer and pleasure is taken in watching that suffering. The fundamental difference between these two types of violence is in the relation to the object, the target. In the sadistic attack it is paramount that the object should not be destroyed, but be preserved in order to be seen to suffer. The object is not eliminated, but controlled. The impact on the victim of a self-preservative attack is irrelevant once the threat to the attacker's survival has been removed.

Stan recognized, after the attack, that he felt absolutely no regret or guilt about what he had done to Grummond and hated himself "for not doing the job properly and finishing him off. For Stan the person and the threat were synonymous. While Grummond existed he posed a threat. Although Stan's violence was essentially self-preservative and as such served a defensive function, it should be perceived as a sign of disturbance. As we learn more about Stan we will see that his attack fulfilled a fantasy that was based on a violent image of who he was as a man. This fantasy, or ego ideal, like its fulfilment in action, functioned to protect Stan from primitive anxieties that were heightened by conflicts associated with adolescence.

The development of the ego ideal

The ego ideal develops in response to the discovery that we are not who we thought we were. As children we learn, to our great disappointment, that we are not the centre of the universe. Our real selves are not omnipotent. Reality disabuses us of the fantasy that we are universally and unconditionally loved. This coincides with inklings that a more powerful person, mother, is somehow responsible for our illusion of self-sufficiency. In an effort to overcome a breakdown in the earliest infant–mother intimacy and restore the illusory relationship with the all-giving mother, the child identifies with and internalizes what Freud referred to as an ego ideal, a kind of role model based on those idealized characteristics of mother, such as omnipotent protection, nourishment and comfort, that the child would like to possess. Later, the father also becomes a role model for the ego ideal as the child separates and individuates itself from the mother. In latency and adolescence the individual chooses other role models from real or fictional, private or public "heroes", or collective ideals. In this way the ego ideal, or role model, develops to help the child as a defence against the normal fears and anxieties associated with being a child: the prospect of separation from or loss of parental love, fears of castration or extinction, loss of control of self and others, sexual impotence, physical weakness, etc.

The "voice of conscience", our super-ego, is primarily prohibitive, conveying the message, "You may not be like this (i.e., like your father or your mother); you may not do all that he or she does; some things are his or her prerogative." These proscriptions defend parental authority. The ego ideal or role model, on the other hand, is prescriptively incorporating the way to behave in order to satisfy ourselves. Its message is, "I would like to be like this (like mother or father)." The super-ego, in turn, measures our achievements against the standards of the role model. If the ego is deemed to have measured up in thought or deed, there is an increase in self-esteem through a feeling of being loved and protected by the super-ego.[3] Some perverse and/or antisocial behaviour occurs without conflict, prohibition, or guilt because it wins the superego's approval as the fulfilment of a pathological ego ideal. However, failure to reach the ego ideal's standards arouses feelings of criticism and persecution by the super-ego, resulting in inferiority, shame and disgust. You will remember that Stan hated himself "for not doing the job properly" and finishing Grummond off. Material from Stan's weekly psychotherapy sessions with me at the —— Clinic will be used to illustrate the development and function of violence as a defence against breakdown in a male adolescent.

Stan's early childhood

Stan was the first-born son of a violent father and a mother who hated being alone with her baby and had great difficulty cuddling him. Stan would not eat with the family in his early years and was often allowed to take food up to his room. Sometimes Stan panicked when he was eating and could not get his food down. When Stan was four years old, the next sibling, John, was born but died after just one day. The family was unable to mourn this loss. When Stan was told of John's death his mother remembers Stan asking, "Who shot him?" After John's death Stan began rocking. Stan's inability to properly mourn his infant brother's death and resolve his guilt about his death wishes towards John made it impossible for him to separate from his brother and let him go. Instead, Stan internalized his brother as a persecuting figure.[4] Stan told me about a delusion of being occupied by John:

> Whenever I felt in a rage I used to think it was my dead brother
> John's fault. When I was 13 or 14 I thought he was living inside me.

A year after John's death, George was born with a club foot. Three months later Stan started school but had difficulty separating from his mother. He cried a great deal but his mother was preoccupied with meeting the demands of her disabled son. Stan had a repetitive dream during his early days at school of:

. . . being left alone in a lighted classroom waiting for his mother to pick him up. It was getting darker and darker outside and he was all alone. All the children had been picked up by their parents.

He thinks the dream was actually based on real events and it has haunted him for many years.

Stan became phobic about buttons. He hated having them on his clothes. If his mother left buttons around ready to be sewn back on a garment, Stan would confront her in a paranoid fashion saying, "Why did you leave that lying around? Did you do it deliberately?" Stan had been breast-fed with difficulty for three months because his mother had inverted nipples. One can only speculate that the nipple, represented by a button, had become a persecuting object. Meanwhile, Stan and his mother denigrated his violent, under-achieving father. In fact, Stan and his father have regularly come to blows for as long as Stan can remember. In response to his father's actual violence, Stan's perception of his mother as destructive towards her children, her physical withdrawal, the longing, vulner-ability and rage associated with that, guilt about his infant brother's death, and the experience of being displaced by the most formidable rival—a damaged brother—Stan escaped into a comic-book hero.

Ironman

When Stan was four years old his beloved grandfather introduced him to Ironman. Ironman was a comic book hero (Clayton, 1989) whose real name was Tony Stark. Young Stark triggered a booby trap in Vietnam and a piece of shrapnel lodged in his chest. He was captured but had only one week to live before the shrapnel pene-trated his heart. With the help of another prisoner, the renowned Oriental physicist Professor Ho Yinsen, and his laboratory. Stark designed and built a suit of armour with a pacemaker that would keep his heart beating after the shrapnel entered it. Yinsen sacri-ficed his life to give Stark time to become "activated". Stark, as his alter-ego Ironman, avenged Yinsen's death and embarked on a career of combating any force or person who threatened the security of America or the world. When Stark put on Ironman's armour he became impregnable and his strength was magnified to a superhuman level. But for all his power and invincibility, Ironman did not have a fulfilling long-term heterosexual relationship. In fact, Stark was shot and crippled by a former lover who was mentally disturbed. He could, however, still function normally within his Ironman armour!

Stan's identification with Ironman was delusional; he actually believed that he, Stan, was made of steel. Stan wasn't pretending; he was Ironman. When Stan was about seven years old, he had a chest X-ray. Something told him not to look at the X-rays, but he did, and saw "these little ribs, no steel". His dream was shattered and he felt defenceless. Stan went on to say: "I used to pray, when I should have been studying, that I'd be a werewolf because I knew I wasn't Ironman."

The intimate and dangerous mother

As a child Stan would have had to make sense of a mother who produced a baby that was, in Stan's mind, murdered, and who also gave birth to a son with a club foot. Stan chose as his ego ideal a frighteningly powerful and nearly indestructible macho role model which would keep him safe from the object of his desire, a mother who kills and damages her children in her womb. The parental figure that was represented by Ironman is Stan's father.

However, Stan also believed that he had a special relationship with his mother, whom he felt was the only one who understood him. What he enjoyed most was talking with her at night. They both left their bedroom doors open so that they could talk to each other, as Stan put it, "as two voices and no bodies". Stan dealt with his anxieties about being with his intimate but dangerous mother by keeping her at a distance to ensure there was no physical or sexual contact ("no bodies"). As a young boy, Stan's first solution to this conflict was to get inside Ironman, an exaggeratedly masculine identity. Later, Stan relied upon other violent role models to defend against anxieties about incest. Breakdown in adolescence triggered by conflicts associated with the adolescent phase of development takes many forms. I will consider the defensive function of violence in adolescence only in relation to the dangers of heterosexuality and passivity, and in a peripheral way to the risk of suicide.

The adolescent process

The new realities of hormonal and physiological changes initiated by puberty thrust the body's sexuality and musculature to the centre of the psychic stage and create a conflict with earlier self-images. Increasing awareness of erotic sensations in the genitals, enhanced by childhood masturbation, gives the genitals prominence over oral and anal zones of erotic satisfaction, so that the genital comes to dominate the child's sexual image of his body. The establishment of genital dominance enables adolescents to take over responsibility for their bodies from their parents and develop heterosexual relationships with non-incestuous objects. It is not uncommon for an adolescent who is in search of a gender role identity to accommodate and express his developing adult sexuality to identify with contemporary heroes (e.g. pop stars and sports heroes). The adolescent's choice is likely to be influenced by earlier role models, or ego ideals.

The ego ideal with which Stan identified at puberty when his child's body was developing into a man's was a violently destructive android from the film *Blade Runner*. This android was a robot with a human body. The android image of himself, like Ironman, was multidetermined. It reflected Stan's alienation from his new sexual body as well as the concrete way that his violent fantasies influenced his choice of a role model who was alive on the outside but only mechanical on the inside.

Violence as a defence against the dangers of heterosexuality

The male adolescent's impulse to achieve genital gratification in intercourse with women revives prepubertal repressed incestuous wishes, which, in turn, strain earlier defensive solutions. In his therapy, Stan moved back and forth between his infantile wishes to get inside his mother (a residue of the earlier wish for intimacy), and his wishes to establish a heterosexual relationship with a non-incestuous object (stimulated by his emerging adult sexuality).

Stan's conscious sexual fantasies were heterosexual. He usually had one-night stands because of his acknowledged anxiety about "being trapped into being good with these girls if I continue with them". This would disarm him because, as he says, "I only feel safe when I am bad". The task of developing a genital relationship with the opposite sex was problematic because of his fear of being disarmed by women. Although anxieties that he was homosexual, reinforced by shame associated with having engaged in mutual masturbation with some male friends during latency, led Stan to attack men who derided his heterosexuality, the threat to his masculinity came primarily from women. After stamping on the face of a male "yuppie" who insinuated that he was a homosexual. Stan ran back home and bitterly reminded his mother that when he was young she became "mad, dead, and couldn't leave the house". This memory of an emotionally unavailable mother demonstrates the link in Stan's mind between his uncertain masculinity and a mother who couldn't support him. Later that night Stan dreamt that his penis was cut off by a vagina. Wishes to have intercourse with his mother became conscious and acknowledged in his sessions. The lifting of the repression of his incestuous wish aroused anxiety about father's retaliation and fears that he would be trapped inside mother. This resulted in his seeing all women as dangerous. Stan wrote a polymorphous perverse story about a "penis flytrap" from which he managed to extract his bleeding penis with difficulty.

Violence as a defence against excessive passivity

The strength of the passive orientation inherent in excessive child-hood longings will threaten to overwhelm the ill adolescent with despair about being able actively to initiate a move towards geni-tality. Anxieties aroused by taking an active role in heterosexual intercourse, on the one hand, and passive wishes to merge with the woman, on the other, can be illustrated with some material from Stan's psychotherapy. Early in a session Stan told me that he elected to stay the night with Betty, his girlfriend, when his mates left the pub. He got drunk with Betty and then went back to her flat for sex. After intercourse he dreamt of:

Grace Jones (a pop singer and movie star who presents herself as a dangerous phallic woman). He mounted her and then woke up with a start. When he went back to sleep he dreamt about Grace Jones mounting him.

Stan went on to say that the next night he had another dream about:

> ... getting his mate Paul out of hospital. They wouldn't let Stan leave and took his clothes. He grabbed a bathrobe, put it on, ran down corridors and crawled through ventilation ducts to get outside and away. But then he had no money.

I linked the second dream to coming along to see me today and wondered if it was related to his disappointment with me last week and his expressed belief that only a residential setting, the hospital in the dream, could help him. I added that being held, as in the hospital, also carried with it the threat of being trapped. I wondered if today he was worried about being trapped by me. I thought the dream also disguised a pleasure in escaping into a woman just as he had begun the session by telling me he had gone off to have sex with Betty rather than going to a nightclub with his mates.

Stan associated to:

> ... how Paul says he is his best mate but Stan can't say it back. Paul "slags off" his cousin by disparaging his penis as too small. He remembers how his ex-mates always knocked girls. He was slagged off because he was the only one in his group who got laid. Some of the other guys went out with younger girls and he thinks it's repulsive. He can recall his own fear of being seen as "queer" [gay] by others when he is out with his mates. Perhaps that was why he wanted to get away from them. He wondered if they're queer. [He was beginning to get quite angry; his face reddening, his muscles tensing and his breath coming in shorter gasps.]

I took up his anxiety about his own masculinity and suggested that he shifted his insecurity on to his mates and then saw them as envious of him.

In following the sequence of material as it emerged in the session, it appeared that his dreams of Grace Jones, which occur after having sex with Betty, represented an attempt to gratify a sexual wish that also aroused anxiety when he penetrated Betty. When he assumed the dominant position with Grace Jones, that anxiety became unbearable, interrupted the dream and he awoke. However, anxiety did not interrupt sleep when he dreamt of assuming a passive feminine posture with Grace Jones. The session

seemed to reflect Stan's anxiety about being active with a dangerous phallic woman. Grace Jones, retreating to a male (Paul) who
belittled another man (by turning him into a boy with a "too small
penis") and regressing to an infantile relationship (getting inside
the mother/hospital) from which he must escape. The consequence
of this regression was the loss of his potency (ending up without
any money) if he actually succeeded in returning to mother's womb
(losing his clothes and crawling through ventilation ducts), and an
increase in his homosexual anxiety if he gave up his penis in favour
of a passive asexual relationship with his mother. The shift in the
material from a dangerous phallic woman to a man who is not so
much castrating as narcissistically wounding (i.e., turning him into
a little boy) represented Stan's experience of his mother and father.
Stan was in a bind. To become active and penetrative with a woman
aroused castration anxiety. But to surrender to a passive role with a
woman confirmed his feeling of helplessness and passivity, feelings
which he equated with being like a baby again. Stan's violence
stood between the threats posed by heterosexuality, on the one
hand, and regression and breakdown on the other hand. Violence
enabled him to maintain a precarious foothold in adolescence. As
he said: "If I wasn't violent, I would cry like a baby."

Violence, perhaps more than any other delinquent act, compels
the environment to manage the adolescent (Winnicott, 1956). In fact,
Stan's violence alerted the police and the courts to his need for
holding and containment, although neither Stan nor the authorities
were aware of Stan's unconscious need of a father who would
contain him while protecting him from a mother he feared would
take him over (Fonagy & Target, 1995). A similar dynamic appears
in presuicidal states, when "the internalized father's failure to inter-
vene in the pathological mother/child relationship . . . [becomes]
. . . most critical" (Campbell, 1995, p. 320).

Violence as a defence against suicide

When a violent adolescent's projection on to another person fails,
that adolescent is liable to relate to his own body as an object upon
which to project unacceptable wishes or anxieties. When this occurs
the adolescent's body becomes a target for his violence and there is

a risk of suicide. It is not uncommon for murderers to try to kill themselves after they have been incarcerated, i.e., after external restriction has rendered violence against others inoperative. As Stan became able to understand his violent fantasies in therapy and think before attacking people, his paranoid ideation was more difficult to maintain and he turned his aggression against himself. During his therapy, Stan entered presuicide states, i.e., periods when his body had become expendable and he had a conscious plan to kill it. Initially, Stan's suicide fantasy had two components: a revenge motive and the fulfilment of his wish to merge with his mother. The revenge motive first appeared in the transference as his retaliation for my not helping him. At another level, suicide represented Stan's way back to his mother, a delusional psychic reunion with her from which Stan could never be separated. He was terrified by the thought that she might die first. He said life wouldn't be worth living and he would have to kill himself in order to join her. His suicide fantasy was also, in part, an identification with his mother, who had been suicidal herself at one time.

As the revenge motives and wishes to merge with mother were analysed, the content of Stan's suicide fantasies changed to include the wish to eliminate his body because it was seen as the source of dirty infantalizing homosexual fantasies (Laufer & Laufer, 1984). For a time Stan was convinced that the only way he could find relief from these tormenting thoughts was to destroy his brain. These fantasies subsided when Stan was able to think about his wishes and fears of being dependent on me, when he found therapy helpful.

Discussion

Stan has had no parent to hide behind. Mother did not protect him from a violent father. Father did not stand in the way of Stan's wish to merge with mother. Although Stan retained strong pregenital wishes, he did not develop a perversion nor did he attempt suicide. Instead he identified with his father's violence and compensated for the lack of a protecting masculine figure in his life by eroticizing nearly indestructible phallic ego ideals. However, this left Stan perilously close to homosexual fantasies of submission to a man's penis.

From the age of four through adolescence Stan had a delusional belief that his violence or the threat of it could protect him from paranoid anxieties (about men and women) as it did his heroes. Stan's violent fantasies were highly gratifying in themselves. As he recounted them to me during sessions his face became flushed, he began panting and his body tensed. Stan became increasingly excited and agitated until he would describe in detail the finale of his violent retaliation against known or unknown objects, or himself, after which he would slump back in his chair exhausted and drained, but calm. Although these eroticized ego ideals protected Stan from breakdown, they did not enable him to develop more sophisticated defences or adapt himself to reality. Stan's adolescence was spent in a precarious state. He had not internalized aspects of his father which would enable him to become a separate and independent man. Nor was he helped by his ego ideals, Ironman and the androids, who were violently destructive bodies like father, but lacked heart and soul, free choice, and any hetero-sexual relationships. However, Stan's identification with *Blade Runner* reflects some hope that he can survive the risk of loss asso-ciated with heterosexual affection and attachment. The androids in *Blade Runner* have been preprogrammed to function, or "live", for only a specifically limited period of time, and rebel in an attempt to override their built-in self-destructive mechanism. All of them fail, except for a female android who develops feelings and falls in love with a human.

Notes

1   My view of violence is influenced by participation in The Portman Clinic's research study of the nature of the violent act (Glasser, 1994).
2   Perelberg (1995) also views violence as a reaction to traumatic threats to physical or psychological survival.
3   My view of the super-ego and ego ideal are influenced by Glasser's (1978) characterization of the prescriptive super-ego on the one hand and the prescriptive super-ego in which Glasser incorporates the ego ideal on the other hand . However, I follow Freud's (1921) early model by maintaining a separation between the super-ego and

ego ideal. For a discussion of the distinctions between the super-ego, the ego idea, the ideal self and the ideal object, which is beyond the scope of this paper, I refer the reader to Sandler *et al.*, (1963).

4   A. H. Williams (1965) describes a similar phenomenon in which an undigested psychic trauma is encapsulated and unmetabolized until a victim becomes delusionally identified with the original tormentor, thereby triggering an assault.

References

Blade Runner (1982). Film. Ridley Scott (Director), USA.

Campbell, D. (1995). The role of the father in a pre-suicide state. in *International Journal of Psycho-analysis, 76*: 315–23.

Clayton, B. (1989). Ironman. *The Official Handbook of the Marvel Universe, 3*(4): 10–13.

Fonagy, P., & Target, M. (1995). Understanding the violent patient: the use of the body and the role of the father. *International Journal of Psycho-analysis, 76*(3): 487–501.

Freud, S. (1921). Group psychology and the analysis of the ego. *S.E. 18*, Hogarth and The Institute of Psycho-Analysis.

Glasser, M. (1978). The role of the superego in exhibitionism, *International Journal of Psycho-analysis, 7*: 333–352.

Glasser, M. (1994). Violence: a psychoanalytical research project. *Journal of Forensic Psychiatry, 5*(2): 311–320.

Laufer, M. & Laufer, M. E. (1984). *Adolescence and Developmental Breakdown*, Yale University.

Perelberg, R. (1995). Violence in children and young adults: a review of the literature and some new formulations. *Bulletin of the Anna Freud Centre, 18*: 89–122.

Sandler, J., Holder, A., & Meers, D. (1963). The ego ideal and the ideal self. *Psychoanalytic Study of the Child, 18*: 139–58.

Sohn, L. (1995). Unprovoked assaults—making sense of apparently random violence. *International Journal of Psycho-analysis, 76*(3): 565–575.

Walker, N. (1991). Dangerous mistakes. *British Psychiatry, 158,*: 752–757.

Williams, A. H. (1965). Treatment of abnormal murders. *Howard Journal of Penology, 11*(4): 286–296.

Winnicott, D. (1956). The anti-social tendency. Reprinted in *Collected Papers: Through Paediatrics to Psychoanalysis*, Tavistock (1958).

CHAPTER TWO

Working with suicidal adolescents

Catalina Bronstein

"A deeply depressed 67-year-old woman suffering from a very painful atypical facial neuralgia that did not fit into any clear medical diagnosis was referred for a psychiatric consultation. After discussing her symptoms she described a recent X-ray which had revealed that a small bullet was lodged in her skull. She explained that this had brought back to her the memory that at the age of 16 she had shot herself in the mouth. When asked why she had done such a thing she just shrugged her shoulders and said 'I don't know. I was angry I suppose, so I got the gun and shot myself. Just being childish'."

Carpinacci *et al.*, 1979

This patient's view of her own suicidal attempt might not be very different from the way in which many adolescents who attempt suicide are sometimes viewed by parents, by health workers and by themselves. The anxiety stirred up by some adolescents' strong wishes to attack themselves, often with the clear intention of ending their lives, can lead to the denial of the seriousness of such an action and of the ill health of the adolescents who resort to it. Before starting to examine the issues underlying attempted suicide in adolescence, I would like to stress, as many different authors have done (e.g. Friedman *et al.*, 1972; Crumley, 1982; Joffe, 1989a; Laufer, 1993) that a suicide attempt is always a sign of severe pathology. When trying to understand the possible causes and meaning of attempted suicide in adolescence, one is often left with a number of questions that are not easily answered, such as why would somebody want to end their own life and attempt suicide; and why specifically in adolescence; and furthermore, why is it so difficult to help these adolescents even when one is willing to recognize their need for help?

I will try to explore some of the possible answers to these questions in this chapter, knowing that my exposition will be far from complete. My approach to this subject will focus on the adolescents' state of mind, thus neglecting other important contributors to the suicidal act, such as sociological and family factors.

Adolescence

Before looking at the specific issues of death and suicide, I will begin with a few words about adolescence in general. The age at which adolescence starts varies considerably, as puberty, i.e. the period of life when procreation becomes possible, can also vary. The onset of adolescence is usually marked by a spurt in physical growth that continues until maturation is complete. I am talking of an approximate age span of 12/13 to 22/23 years. There are differences between the experiences of an early adolescent and those of a late adolescent. For example, the impact that the menarche, or first period, has on a 13-year-old girl is different from the way she will experience her periods and her femininity at 18; or the way a 14-year-old boy feels when he is with girls might not be the same as at 20, when he might feel under pressure from peers to have sexual intercourse. Despite these differences, I will address myself to some characteristics that I think are present throughout adolescence.

This period is characterized by the different tasks and needs that the adolescent has to face in order to move into adulthood (Blos, 1962). According to Freud (1905), "with the arrival of puberty, changes set in which are destined to give infantile sexual life its final . . . shape". Klein (1922) also stresses the importance that "the tempestuous uprush of instincts arising at puberty" has, and, when describing the pubertal boy's struggles, she speaks of his need to "achieve an inner detachment from the incestuous links to his mother, though these will remain the foundation and model for later love". She adds that, in order to promote development, a measure of "external detachment from [the] fixation to [the] parents is also necessary".

The prepubertal child's image of him/herself has to give way to take into account a changing body, a mature sexual body that heralds the arrival of a new identity, new freedom and new responsibilities. Irreversible sexual development and the accompanying changes in their bodies give rise to a changing image of themselves as well as a changing image of their parents.

The capacity to face these changes will be influenced greatly by specific psychological characteristics established during childhood. These changes and their accompanying anxieties evoke again the intense experiences and anxieties of early infancy. Such experiences, which in the main have been successfully repressed, now reawaken in a radically new setting, that of a sexually mature body. Difficulties in facing and working through these changes can sometimes lead to intense feelings of despair and hopelessness, which can, in turn, bring about the belief that death is the only possible solution to these conflicts.

What do we mean by death?

Conscious thoughts about death are not infrequent in adolescence. Most adolescents entertain, at some point or other, the wish to kill themselves, to disappear, to see their parents dead. In his work *Thoughts on War and Death*, Freud (1915) says:

> It is indeed impossible to imagine our own death; and whenever we attempt to do so we can perceive that we are in fact still present as spectators. Hence the psychoanalytical school could venture on the assertion that at bottom no one believes in his own death, or, to put the same thing in another way, that in the unconscious every one of us is convinced of his own immortality.

Later, however, Freud adds that, in the unconscious, that attitude is opposed by another which does acknowledge death as the annihilation of life, and he sees death wishes towards others linked to this. 'Indeed, our unconscious will murder even for trifles" (*ibid.*). He then adds (*ibid.*):

Just as for the primaeval man, so also for our unconscious, there is one case in which the two opposing attitudes towards death, the one which acknowledges it as the annihilation of life and the other which denies it as unreal, collide and come into conflict. This case is the same as in primal ages: the death, or the risk of death of someone we love . . . these loved ones are on the one hand an inner possession, components of our own ego; but on the other hand they are partly strangers, even enemies . . . To sum up: our unconscious is just as inaccessible to the idea of our own death, just as murderously inclined towards strangers, just as divided (that is ambivalent) towards those we love . . .

"To be dead" has a specific meaning for each adolescent who attempts suicide, based not only on their conscious reasons for why they wanted to be dead but also mainly on the unconscious phantasies that underlay their thinking and actions. For example, death can represent an omnipotent idealized union with a dead parent. This was the case for a 17-year-old girl, M, whose mother had died when she was 11.

M kept a very idealized image of her mother, whilst feeling abandoned at a time when she felt she most needed her. She could not establish a good relation with either her father or stepmother and felt she could not allow herself to have friends, to enjoy being alive. She became very depressed and suicidal after puberty. M could not understand this as there were no "real" reasons why she should feel so guilty when her mother's death had not been caused by her actions. Whenever she thought of death she felt it was like being somewhere extremely peaceful. She longed to go to sleep and never wake up.

The idea of death is often idealized as promising "a Nirvana state of freedom from desire, disturbance and dependence" (Rosenfeld, 1957, in Spillius, 1994).

In some very disturbed adolescents, death can be the end result of a compelling action to get rid of a part of themselves that is felt to represent negative characteristics (such as attacking a part of their bodies felt as "evil" or "bad"), and an attempt to silence internal persecuting voices which torment them. This was the case for N, an 18-year-old boy who jumped from a first-floor window trying to escape from accusing voices. The fact that the idea of "death" can be the expression of very diverse phantasies does not imply that some attempted suicides should be considered more "real" or "valid" than others. All are indicative of serious disturbance, and can potentially lead to actual death.

The adolescents' movement towards feeling in charge of their sexuality and the process of establishing a new identity and responsibilities induces a renegotiation of the roles of both parents and children. The awareness of bodily changes and the experience of the development of the body into a sexually mature one confronts the adolescent with the reality of the passing of time and the inevitability of death. Puberty also reawakens the vivid awareness of the sexual relationship between the parents and contempt for it as well as hatred of being excluded from it. According to Pirlot-Petroff (1989), suicide can then become the search for a narcissistic immortality that defies the notion of the finite as linked to sexuality.

The need to reconcile infantile omnipotent phantasies and desires with the current reality thus comes to the fore. Triumphant feelings linked to the experience of youth, of strength, of feeling they have a boundless world and endless time in front of them, can easily alternate with a painful awareness of the passing of time. A sense of loss and feelings of being lost, insecure, unloved and unlovable, as well as anxiety about parental deaths or their own vulnerability and mortality, can easily assail them.

In facing the loss of the infantile body and infantile identity, the adolescent is now left exposed to the possibility that his omnipotent phantasies, whether violent or sexual, could be realized. The anger, the hatred of the parents and the wish to attack them, which were moderately safe in childhood when the omnipotence of such feelings could not possibly be matched by the capacity to really kill the parent, become dangerously possible for the adolescent, who now experiences that he could actually damage the parent. In the same way, love, when accompanied by sensuous feelings or incestuous phantasies and seductive games, can also be experienced now as dangerous, potentially leading to actual, real intercourse with a parent. Therefore, intense feelings, both of love and hatred, are often experienced in adolescence as likely to lead to action, to be unstoppable and uncontrollable. Being out of control is equated by the adolescent with the experience of being driven mad, and this might partly explain the increased need to resort to defence mechanisms to deal with these anxieties, such as regression, splitting, projective identification, dissociation, which thus become intensified in adolescence.

The different feelings experienced by adolescents towards their parents and towards themselves are interpreted in the context of this highly sensitive, changeable, at times desperately intense, atmosphere that is experienced by them both in the internal world and in the relationship with the actual parents. Adolescents frequently feel (that they have to keep these uncontainable, maddening feelings and phantasies to themselves, as they feel too ashamed to share them and certainly feel them to be unique. Humiliation, embarrassment and shame can be experienced as overwhelming, and can lead to a retreat into themselves, making them feel even more at the mercy of their own impulses. It is at these times that peer groups become very important. They provide an environment in which these intense feelings can be shared and on to which they can be projected, and they help the adolescent in the significant move away from living in the parental world to one where new relationships can be established.

The struggle with maturing sexuality

The emotional impact that bodily changes have on adolescents can induce in them the belief that it is their bodies that are responsible for their misery. The body, which can bring intense pleasure often accompanied by anxiety and guilt, is one of the main foci of preoccupation in adolescence. The adolescent boy who experiences erections, has wet dreams and feels compelled to masturbate, as well as the girl who feels compelled to look at her body and check the size of her breasts, her weight, the way she looks, and the wish to touch her genitals or be touched, may often feel at the mercy of their body. Deluded ideas such as "the problem is that my nose is too big" or "if only I lost weight everything will be all right" or "if I could develop a more muscular body ... " are certainly not infrequent. This can also tell us that the adolescent may identify a part of his/her body as "bad" or "wrong", containing all the rejected and unlovable aspects of him/herself, which the adolescent may then feel needs concretely to be removed or changed in order to regain the lost peace of mind (Cardon, 1989; Joffe, 1989a; Laufer & Laufer, 1984).

> A 16-year-old girl felt she was the victim of accusations she heard coming from everywhere, voices shouting that they knew she was a "bitch", "evil", "bad" etc. The accusations developed not very long after her first sexual intercourse. Her mother was a schizophrenic, now under medication, and the two of them lived together on their own. The girl said she knew that her mother was ill when she was pregnant with her and that the doctors had said she should get rid of the baby. The daughter. A, had often thought her mother might stab her at night and at one point she told me she had wanted to ran away from her mother, and she whispered this as if the mother, who was not in the room, might hear her. A felt extremely anxious and needed to wash herself very frequently because of what she felt had been left inside her from the sexual intercourse. Washing herself compulsively did not seem to ease her anxiety and she developed the idea that in order to feel all right she needed to stab herself in the belly. She confirmed my interpretation that she thought there was a baby that had to be killed, even though she also knew that she could not possibly be pregnant.

It would be tempting to explore in some detail what the killing of this imaginary baby may have meant to this girl.[1] She felt identified with the baby in its evil and badness. She decided that it had to be got rid off. At the same time. while she described it, she sounded as if she felt she could concretely get rid of this bad, sexual, evil baby-belly without actually killing herself.

The adolescents' capacity to deal with anxiety depends on their inner resources. These develop from the early relationship with their parents, modified by the child's own unconscious phantasies (configuring an internal representation of the parents or "internal objects"). Rosenfeld (1952) summarizes Klein's understanding of the infant's early relationships:

> She [Klein] has found that, by projecting his libidinal and aggressive impulses on to an external object which at first is his mother's

breast, the infant creates images of a good and a bad breast. These two aspects of the breast are introjected and contribute both to the ego and the superego.

In these early stages, which Melanie Klein called the "schizoid-paranoid position":

> ... there is an inter-relationship between these good and bad objects in that, if the bad objects are extremely bad and persecutory, the good objects as a reaction-formation will become extremely good and highly idealized. Both the ideal objects and the persecutory objects contribute to the early superego ... (*ibid.*)

This position is followed by a move towards integration, conforming to what Klein called "the depressive position" (Steiner, 1993) where:

> ... whole objects begin to be recognized and ambivalent impulses become directed towards the primary object ... These changes result from an increased capacity to integrate experiences and lead to a shift in primary concern from the survival of the self to a concern for the object upon which the individual depends.

According to Britton (1989), ". . . it has become increasingly evident that the capacity to comprehend and relate to reality is contingent on working through the depressive position". He also reminds us that Klein "emphasized that the Oedipus complex develops hand-in-hand with the developments that make up the depressive position . . . " (*ibid.*). The impact that maturing sexuality and Oedipal conflicts have on the adolescent's mind often intensifies anxieties and defences that correspond to the schizoid-paranoid position. As a consequence, there can be an increase in paranoid anxiety and an intensification of defences characteristic of the schizoid-paranoid position, such as splitting, projective identification, denial and idealization. This is the time when a vulnerable child who more or less managed to go through childhood without causing great alarm to parents and teachers might feel unable to deal with the oncoming changes. But it is also the time when psychotherapeutic intervention can really offer great help, however difficult it is for the desperate adolescent to accept the help that is provided by the same adult world that he or she both admires and hates.

One could also say that what I have described is part of most adolescents' history and that not all of them attempt suicide. Conscious thoughts and wishes to be dead are quite frequent, but what makes it possible for an adolescent to act on those wishes and attempt to destroy him/herself? I should emphasize that this area of study is far from being thoroughly explored and understood. I will confine myself to trying to understand the psychodynamic factors involved in these actions as well as the difficulties that arise in the treatment of these young people. In no sense am I denying the importance of other factors such as early trauma, social causes, parental disturbances and sexual abuse. I will next describe a clinical example which may help to understand some aspects of attempted suicide in adolescence.

Clinical case: Sally

A 15-year-old girl whom I shall call Sally was referred by her school to our Walk-In Centre. Teachers were worried by her playing truant, her apparent state of depression, her not being able to stay for long inside the classroom. The school put a lot of pressure on her to come to our Centre. She attended during school hours as her parents did not agree to the referral and denied there was any problem with their daughter. Sally came to the first interview with a friend from school. She told me later she did not like to go anywhere on her own. She was rather overweight, looking young for her age. She was dressed in a quite scruffy and untidy school uniform that was too large for her. She also wore a long coat, which she did not take off, as if trying to cover herself up with it. She barely looked at me. Sally mumbled and fidgeted with the edge of her coat. She told me that the school Head had wanted her to come and she was quite upset by this as she had built a very strong relation to this teacher, who now seemed unable to go on helping Sally on her own. Sally seemed to feel betrayed and let down by the referral. She reluctantly told me about difficulties at home, that she had to look after a younger sister when her mother left for work. She also talked about her father, whom she experienced as very distant, quite unreachable, and towards whom she felt very negative. She was clearly resentful about having to talk to me and when I took this up she just remained silent.

However, Sally did respond to my wondering about suicidal ideas and she said that if she had more courage she would certainly have killed herself by now. She then told me she had a boyfriend and had gone out with him just twice because his friends teased him about going out with her. Now the whole school was talking about it and he had decided to end the relationship. She said she did not mind this as she did not like him anyway. She added that she did not trust anybody. She just did not care about anything, and she did not care whether she was alive or dead. The only thing she did feel positive about was that she had a group of three very close girl friends, with whom she spent most of her time.

Sally came three more times but not consecutively. She did not come for her next appointment. I wrote to her offering another one. On her third visit, five weeks after the first one, she brought some photographs she wanted to show me: of her dog [she later said that he was the only thing, together with her friends, that kept her alive because she could not think of anybody else looking after him], and of her mother, who, by contrast with her, looked very beautiful, feminine and well dressed. There was also a photograph of her grandfather's grave but she could not explain how it got mixed up with the others. There were no photographs of herself. She said she really disliked the way she looked but she was very pleased at how her mother looked. The photograph of her grandfather's grave led her to talk about death and spiritualism. She told me that she and her three friends got together to try to contact the dead. It was clear that the whole thing was making her feel very anxious but was also exciting and made her feel powerful at the same time. This was followed by more missed appointments. (I should explain here that the interviews we offer at the —— Adolescent Centre are initial exploratory meetings with the adolescent. We take the time we feel is necessary to understand the adolescent and what sort of help he or she needs. This can take from four or five interviews to several months. There is no fixed contract at this point and each meeting is arranged by common agreement with the adolescent.)

Sally did not turn up for her next appointment but sent me a little notebook in the post. It said:

My thoughts are the only things that keep me going, as well as my
friends trying to cheer me up and comfort me but it's no good. I know
deep down I am not wanted. I am stupid, I can't do anything right. I
wish something would happen to take me away from this horrible
world. Sometimes I feel my friends hate my guts and they wish I'd go.
I feel the need to be alone and want to be free. Today I had an argument with my parents and they must really hate me all of them. Parents
sure know how to make you depressed. Today they kept saying you
are getting too heavy. You are even bigger than your mother now. I
know I am fat and useless but I do wish they would not keep rubbing
it in.

This was followed by a description of the rows at home between
her parents, her feelings of hatred towards her father, her jealousy
of her sister and feelings that her mother did not care for or love her
and how the only way she could sleep was to hold an old doll of
hers. She then wrote:

Some people are violent, it's lucky I believe in that stuff about reincar-
nation and life after death.

She missed the next two appointments and, thinking that she
was at risk, I liaised with the school (she had given me permission
to do so) and spoke to her teacher, who was also very concerned
about her, but her parents did not want anybody else involved and
Sally felt she could not go against their wishes.

Sally did not return until after she had made a suicidal attempt
at school and had been referred back to us by her GP. Her description of the attempt was that she had had a row with her three
closest friends, who, she felt, had ganged up against her. She said
they started bullying her. Sally had gone to seek protection from her
Head of Year and when she came out of the room, the girls, who
had followed her, started shouting at her. She could not remember
at this point what it was that her friends were saying. She could
only remember that she had gone into a room and taken all the pills
she had in a bottle given to her by her GP for chest congestion. She
then went to the next lesson. The teacher realized she was unwell
and she was taken to hospital in an ambulance and had her stom-
ach pumped out. Later on she remembered what it was that her
friends had shouted that had precipitated the overdose: it was that

they were sorry for her, her life was not worth living, basically, that she should kill herself.

After the suicidal attempt. Sally came back looking very detached, cut off, far more than when I started seeing her. She said that was the way she had felt while she was taking the pills: no feelings, no thoughts. However, despite her detachment, I was surprised by her reaction to one of my comments about her plans after leaving school: she smiled in a rather superior way and contemptuously added: "Well, it is not in my plans to be around at that time!"

The suicidal attempt was followed by her account of other self-destructive behaviour that had gone on beforehand as well, which she felt very disturbed by but she could not talk about. She told me that she felt compelled to cut her arms at times, to binge and vomit, and to drink alcohol. It took a long time, about two years of work, for this girl to be able to accept that she needed intensive help, and for her parents to agree to it.

Sally's internal world

In looking at this material I will necessarily have to neglect some very important issues such as her actual family relationships and the resistance to the acknowledgement of the need for psychological help, the whole process of referral and details about this girl's early life.

I will only say that she seemed always to have been a rather vulnerable, very sensitive and jealous girl, extremely attached to the mother, whom she thought of as very beautiful, attractive, outgoing. She had very strong ambivalent feelings of envy, jealousy, and love towards her. These feelings were experienced in a very split way. She had always found separations, principally from her mother, very difficult. As a child she had not wanted to go to school and was frequently ill, forcing her mother to give up work in order to look after her. However, Sally had not been involved in self-destructive behaviour until after puberty. Puberty seems to have thrown Sally into turmoil. The idealized relationship she had had with her mother during childhood was now more difficult to sustain. Sally was now confronted by her own sexual development as a woman. This brought intense conflict between her own sexual needs and desires and the feelings aroused by the awareness of her mother's sexuality, which was now more difficult to deny. Her hostility towards her mother and towards herself for containing these feelings of hatred made her feel guilty and despise herself. Her criticisms and hatred were projected on to her body, making her perceive herself as disgusting and bad. They were also projected on to her father, who was therefore seen as the one to be blamed for her not being able to have a really good relationship with her mother. At the same time she felt pressured by her friends to "behave" like a woman, to have a boyfriend. Despite having sexual feelings towards boys at times, she also projected her hostility on to them and saw them as stupid and useless, even though she was not aware of what she actively did to make them reject her. She felt mainly interested in being loved by a woman, thus attracting more self-criticisms as she felt inadequate and abnormal.

According to Rosenfeld (1952), ". . . if the bad objects are extremely bad and persecutory, the good objects as a reaction formation will become extremely good and highly idealized". Sally kept the figure of her mother as highly idealized, and denigrated both herself and her father [she later told me that she felt she resembled her father physically and that her mother would always stress this as a criticism of the way she looked]. She could not bear even to think about her hostility towards her mother, and her mother's refusal to support treatment was denied and blamed solely on her father. The idealization of her mother was transferred to other women, such as her teachers, to some of whom she became passionately attached, and, later on, to her friends. Closeness to a woman, such as she had managed to establish first with her Head of Year and was later to experience with me, filled her with relief and hope, but also with anxiety about homosexual wishes that made her feel sexually abnormal. She said it was terrible for her to feel that her "friends or the Head of Year and their love mattered more than anything in the world". At the same time she had attempted to have a relationship with a boy. Its failure, which she had actively but unconsciously provoked, threw her into more despair.

Sally blamed her body, which she tortured, as the, source of her distress. Her hated body was one that contained, in phantasy, the identification with the hated aspects of the rival-father and her wish to identify herself with the object desired by her mother. At the same time, whenever she looked at herself, her fully developed female body made her acutely aware of the impossibility of sustaining the phantasy of being the one who could satisfy her mother's desire. Sally's hatred of her body, to which she attributed all sort of negative qualities, made her see herself as bad, ugly, fat, disgusting and worthless of any love, and drove her to attacking herself in various ways. The intense hatred of the body in suicidal adolescents has been stressed by authors such as Joffe (1989b), Kernberg (1974), Laufer (1993), and Pedinelli (1989).

Sally felt temporarily relieved by the self-punishment (such as cutting herself) but the hatred contained in this led to more guilt and condemnation, and to more feelings of disgust and hatred towards herself and her internal objects. This intensified her compelling need for more attacks on herself, thus throwing her into a state of despair where destructiveness was felt to be out of control, as she felt trapped in this sado-masochistic relationship with herself. In this, Sally was far from unique. Many adolescents are drawn into this vicious circle and consider suicide as an escape from it. At these times they experience an enormous sense of hopelessness, as they feel unlovable and unloved. They crave love and help but their need for it, and the strong feelings attached to dependency, jealousy and envy, provoke more hatred and guilt and set in motion the sado-masochistic cycle from which they cannot free themselves. At these moments the idea of suicide seems to offer immense relief.

The suicidal attempt

It was not apparent that Sally had a secret plan about how and when she would kill herself. Some adolescents do have a secret plan and set themselves time limits by which they must prove to themselves and others that they can master what they believe is the cause of their depression, such as, for example, to succeed in their studies, to have a girlfriend or to reduce their weight. Hawton & Catalan (1987) suggest that premeditation is often associated with serious suicidal intention. Some adolescents hold on for the rest of their lives to the idea that committing suicide may be a solution to their conflicts.

Sally's attempts to deal with her anxiety about her destructiveness, and the failure to ease guilt and repair the damage she felt she was doing to her internal objects, led to more splitting of good and bad, and to a desperate need to keep a good part of herself, like the good loving and caring friends, separate from any hostile feelings. In that idealization of her friends—as with her teacher, and as, I think, earlier with her mother—she projected her hatred, jealousy, competitiveness and envy on to the "others", who were excluded from the group or from the very intense partnership that seemed to make her and her friends inseparable and all good. However, Sally was permanently exposed to the breaking down of this defensive system. Her teacher had not been able to cope with her and "betrayed" her by referring her to us, and her friends turned against her. She was therefore left having to deal with the hatred and despair she perceived in herself towards the mother–teacher–friend, who was experienced to be abandoning her. I am implying here that her friends were suddenly perceived as containing the contempt and hatred that Sally was already feeling towards the woman in herself and mirroring the accusations that she was making to herself and to the internalized mother. Her friends' statement that Sally's life was not worth living and that she should be dead felt like an echo of what her self-punishing super-ego was already telling her. Her attempted suicide can be described using Fenichel's (1946) description of suicide as "an act of rebellion and murder of the original objects incorporated in the superego". Freud (1920) wrote, in relation to suicide:

> Probably no one finds the mental energy to kill himself unless, in the first place, in doing so he is at the same time killing an object with whom he has identified himself.

At that crucial moment which led to the attempt. Sally killed off in her mind any good aspects of herself and any loved and loving aspects of her objects. If she had kept them alive she would have had to face conflict, anxiety and guilt about what she was going to do and would have probably stopped herself. She would even have remembered her dog, which she could not bear to leave behind. What enabled her to go ahead with the suicidal attempt was the destruction of her capacity to think, to make links with any good aspects of herself and of her internal objects. She therefore cut off from what she was doing and mechanically swallowed pill after pill. During a suicidal attempt, adolescents undergo a process of dissociation leading to depersonalization. This is what enables them to go ahead with it (Laufer, 1993). This dissociation can be sometimes extreme, particularly in severe suicidal attempts, when the adolescents feel totally removed from reality. However, in this case. Sally had not completely given up and managed to retain some knowledge of what she was doing, some link with reality and with her objects.

It seems important here to bring in a different aspect that may seem to overcomplicate matters. We might ask about the reasons why Sally kept on rejecting the help that was offered to her, not turning up for her interviews, when, at the same time, she clearly wanted me to know how she felt by posting her notebook to me. And why her mocking comment when I spoke about her future? A feeling of omnipotent gratification is experienced in connection to the suicidal attempt, together with helplessness and despair. This may not be felt during the act, because at such a moment the adolescents feel too numb, too dissociated, but it may be felt before and after the attempt. A frequent phantasy is that the suicidal attempt will make them feel free. It becomes the symbolic equivalent to a separation they feel they cannot achieve, particularly from the mother, and these adolescents may feel they are in now in control of their bodies and their lives.

At the same time, suicide can also be an expression of the wish for a union with the idealized object. *It becomes the equivalent of absolute union and absolute freedom at the same time.* There is, then, in these adolescents, a strong idealization of death that goes together with the denial of its reality. In this omnipotent, deluded way, Sally felt she could decide to die but would go on living, coming back to earth if her friends called her back (which meant that they really wanted her back) and reincarnating into somebody else. She would become absolutely free from her mother, and from her needs and dependence on her as well as from the hatred she felt towards her, and free as well from her body and mind that made her experience those needs. Sally's day-dreams, in which she saw herself as dead, watching her mother crying at her funeral, are an indication that she felt that suicide would guarantee her a permanent place in her mother's mind and at the same time punishing her forever with guilt. Freud's statement, in "The economic problem of masochism" (1924), that ". . . even the subject's destruction of himself cannot take place without libidinal satisfaction", seems to be very relevant.

For all these reasons, these adolescents might actively reject the very help they are desperately longing for. The hatred, envy and contempt of the adult to whom the adolescents have to turn for help, plus the wish to hold on to the idealization and to the phantasy of being in control by entertaining the possibility of killing themselves, makes helping them a very difficult task. There is a demand on the adolescents" part to be taken seriously as well as to deny any seriousness at all. These adolescents hold on to this final solution as a means of feeling in control (Laufer, 1993). At the same time there is gratification in feeling powerful and seeing the therapist carry the anxiety that they cannot bear themselves. Surviving a suicide attempt can make an adolescent feel even more omnipotent and not infrequently one will hear them saying, referring to the attempt, "when I died . . . " or "after I died . . . ".

When treating these adolescents, the analyst usually is left, as I was with Sally, with the feeling that one has to wait not knowing, and to be able to bear not knowing, whether they are going to kill themselves or not, but without giving up hope. The therapist's hopelessness about the possibility of helping these adolescents can be experienced in the same way that Sally experienced her friends—that one is turning against them and confirming their belief that their hatred makes them totally unworthy of love. All this complexity is relived in the relationship to the therapist and care workers. To stay with the anxiety that these adolescents provoke, to empathize with their hopelessness and despair without denying their destructiveness or becoming hopeless ourselves, to avoid colluding with the condemnations of their super-ego and to avoid joining in with the idealization of the magical union through death is a very difficult task.

For all of these reasons I think it is vital for these adolescents to be taken seriously, to get help (if possible, intensive psychoanalytic psychotherapy), but also for the professionals working with them to be able to have a space where they can share their anxieties about these adolescents with colleagues and supervisors. Even though we may fail, it is worth remembering that these desperate adolescents are dependent on our capacity not to give up hope.

Note

1   This example has also appeared in Bronstein & Flanders (1998).

Acknowledgements

I am grateful to Dr Elizabeth Bott Spillius for her helpful comments on the paper. An earlier version was published (in Spanish) in "Vertex" in *Revista Argentina de Psiqiatriá*, 5(15), 1994.

References

Blos, P. (1962). *On Adolescence. A Psychoanalytic Interpretation*. Free Press

Britton, R. (1989). *The Missing Link: Parental Sexuality in the Oedipus Complex*. London: Karnac.

Bronstein, C., & Flanders, S. (1998). The development of a therapeutic space in a first contact with adolescents. *Journal of Child Psychotherapy*, 24(1), 5–35.

Cardon, A.(1989). Corps impure. *Psychologie Médicale*, 21(4), 505.

Carpinacci, J. *et al.* (1979). Neuralgias faciales. Algunas consideraciones acerca de sus determinantes psicologicos. Consecuencias terapeuticas. *Revista Neurologica Argentina*, 5(2/3): 83–87.

Crumley, F. E. (1982). The adolescent suicide attempt: a cardinal symptom of a serious psychiatric disorder. *American Journal of Psychotherapy*, 36(2): 152–165.

Fenichel, O. (1946). *The Psychoanalytic Study of Neurosis*. Routledge

Freud, S. (1905). Three essays on the theory of sexuality. *S.E.*, 7: 135–243. London: Hogarth and The Institute of Psycho-Analysis.

Freud, S. (1915). Thoughts/or the times on war and death. *S.E.*, 4: 275–300. London: Hogarth and The Institute of Psycho-Analysis.

Freud, S. (1920). The psychogenesis of a case of homosexuality in a woman. *S.E., 18*: 147. London: Hogarth and The Institute of Psycho-Analysis.

Freud, S. (1924). The economic problem of masochism, *S.E., 19*: 157. London: Hogarth and The Institute of Psycho-Analysis.

Friedman, M. *et al.* (1972). Attempted suicide and self-mutilation in adolescence: some observations from a psychoanalytic research project. *International Journal of Psycho-analysis, 53*(2): 179–183.

Hawton, K., & Catalan, J. (1987). *Attempted Suicide*. Oxford Medical.

Joffe, R. (1989a). Mary: attempted suicide. A search for alternative paths. In: M. Laufer & M. E. Laufer (Eds.), *Developmental Breakdown and Psychoanalytic Treatment in Adolescence*. Yale University Press.

Joffe, R. (1989b). Work with suicidal adolescents at a Walk-In Centre in Brent. In: S. Rolene & S. Millar (Eds.), *Extending Horizons: Psychoanalytic Psychotherapy with Children, Adolescents and Families*. London: Karnac.

Kernberg, P. (1974). The analysis of a 15½-year-old girl with suicidal tendencies. In: M. Harley (Ed.), *The Analysis and the Adolescent at Work*, Volume 19, pp. 232–67. New York: Quadrangle.

Klein, M. (1922). Inhibitions and difficulties at puberty. In: *Love, Guilt and Reparation*. London: Hogarth, 1985.

Laufer, M. & Laufer, M. E. (1984). *Adolescence and Developmental Breakdown. A Psychoanalytic View*. Yale University Press.

Laufer, M. E. (1993). A five year study of suicidal adolescents. Paper read at a conference on "Suicide in Adolescence", London. Published as: A research study into attempted suicide in adolescence. In: M. Laufer (Ed.), *The Suicidal Adolescent*, pp. 103–18. London: Karnac, 1995.

Pedinelli, J. L. (1989). "Se sui-cider": le corps entre le désir et l'acte. *Psychologic Médicale, 21*(4): 421–425.

Pirlot-Petroff, G. (1989). Suicide: ultime negation de la mortalité/sexualité. *Psychologic Médicale, 21*(4): 440–442.

Rosenfeld, H. (1952). Notes on the psycho-analysis of the super-ego conflict in an acute schizophrenic patient. In: *International Journal of Psycho-analysis, 33*. Reprinted in *Psychotic States*, pp. 63–103. London: Karnac, 1984.

Spillius, E. (1994). Contemporary Kleinian psychoanalysis. H. Schoenhals (Ed.), *Psychoanalytic Inquiry, 14*(3).

Steiner, J. (1993). *Psychic Retreats* (New Library of Psycho-Analysis 19). London: Routledge in association with The Institute of Psycho-Analysis.

CHAPTER THREE

Working with adolescents: a pragmatic view

Abrahão Brafman

Some definitions of adolescence

From a sociobiological point of view, we might say that we have childhood and adulthood with adolescence as the time in between the two. Biology emphasizes hormones and other physical features to characterize the stage of development of each individual, and society has adopted yardsticks that have varied over the years and in different cultures to determine the rights and duties of each person according to his or her chronological age.

In the psychoanalytic world, following Freud's instinct theory, we speak of childhood, latency, adolescence and adulthood. Latency is seen as a period of quiescence, when the instinctual drives that dominated the child's development through the oral, anal, phallic and genital phases of childhood subside, and we find a child who appears not to be under pressure from instinctual urges. Puberty marks the resurgence of instinctual drives and re-evokes in the growing individual a struggle with unconscious instinctual impulses alongside an effort to accommodate the pressures of his environment and from his developing physical endowment. In other words, early identifications with parents and present dependence on them produce child-like feelings and urges, while widening horizons and growing independence lead the adolescent to rebel against them. Adulthood signifies the achievement of some degree of balance between instinctual drives and the forces of reason, i.e., a sense of becoming a responsible social being.

Ernest Jones (1922) put forward the idea that "in the second decennium of life" the individual recapitulates the developments he or she passed in the first five years, adding that the form of this infantile development "to a great extent determines" how he or she negotiates adolescence. This formulation has been followed by most, if not all, later analysts. Anna Freud (1958) provides a sensitive and comprehensive view of adolescence. She discusses in detail the adolescent's attempt to leave childhood behind and to achieve independence from his parents. This leads to quick changes "from one pathological posture to another": this is very different from the adult, whose pathological picture may be recognized and worked with. The difficulty of engaging adolescent patients in treatment is compared by Anna Freud to patients in mourning or in love: because their libido is invested in a real person, available or just lost, little libido is left to invest in the analyst. After a detailed analysis of various defence presentations, Anna Freud stresses that it is normal for youngsters to waver in their struggles with their impulses and the constraints of their consciences. There is reason to worry only when they become fixed in their behaviour and feelings.

Margaret Mahler (1963) postulated a stage of child development that she called the "separation–individuation" phase. This describes the progress a child makes from being at one with mother towards creating some distance from her and establishing his or her own sense of being a separate self. This development is strongly influenced by the mother's capacity to tolerate and foster the child's independence. In childhood, this occurs during the toddler stage when the child becomes able physically to move away from the mother. Following up the idea that adolescence would represent a second attempt at this move from dependence toward independence, Blos (1967) described adolescence as "the second individuation process". Blos emphasized how treating an adolescent helps one to observe the alternating and interacting pictures of his or her view of childhood and of their present world, though now within very different individual, family and social conditions.

Klein's paranoid-schizoid and depressive positions (Segal, 1964) do not constitute developmental phases *sensu strictu*, but emotional configurations that occur at all stages of the individual's life. The paranoid-schizoid position is seen as a more primitive structure, which, upon certain achievements by the individual, can become the depressive position. Whatever their age, individuals can oscillate between one and the other. This being so, adolescence was not seen as a developmental phase as such, but rather another period of life where these two fundamental positions have a role in characterizing youngsters' relationships with their internal and external objects (e.g. Harris, 1965; also Spillius, 1988). More recently, Anderson & Dartington (1998) define adolescence as a developmental stage where the individual tries to leave behind "infant and childhood longings" and moves to adulthood through a complex process of changes that they compare to the work of mourning.

Erikson (1965) followed Freud's formulations but introduced the social environment as a most important factor in the understanding of adolescence. He stressed the role of the adolescent in society and described the period leading up to adulthood as a "moratorium" during which individuals take stock of their achievements and failures and of what is expected of them, before achieving their full adult role in the family and society at large. Society makes allowances to give youngsters time to find their way through the turmoil of late adolescence (e.g. the years spent at university can be seen as a "moratorium"). Erikson warned that:

> ... the danger of this stage is role confusion. Where this is based on a strong previous doubt as to one's sexual identity, delinquent and outright psychotic episodes are not uncommon.

Laufer (1976) defined "three developmental tasks of adolescence" as "the change in the relationship to the oedipal objects, the change in the relationships to contemporaries and the change in attitude to his own body". He later (1978) wrote:

> I would say categorically that illness in adolescence always contains some abnormality in sexual development and functioning ... [i.e., he considers] adolescence pathology to be *a breakdown in the process of integrating the physically mature body as part of the representation of oneself* [original italics].

In his incomparably rich and colourful language, Winnicott (1961a) depicts this period of conflict and change as fundamentally one of individual growth. Whilst the adolescent is invariably seen as a rebel, struggling to find his or her way to independence, Winnicott stresses the vital importance of the adults who accept the challenge and fight back, supporting the youngster in this turmoil. Much as Anna Freud in the paper quoted earlier, here is also a wise emphasis on time: only the passage of time (Winnicott, 1961b, p. 72) allows processes to unfold and reach their goal. in this case for the adolescent to become an adult.

With all our emphasis on the adolescent as an individual, it is important to recognize the fact that a person's adolescence also signifies a major challenge for the parents. They have to "let go" of someone who has taken up vast hours of their life and they need to find a new *modus vivendi*, counting on each other to satisfy needs that have long been covered up by preoccupations with their "child". Anna Freud (1958) puts this poignantly:

> ... it may be [the adolescent's] parents who need help and guid-
> ance so as to be able to bear with him. There are few situations in
> life which are more difficult to cope with than an adolescent son or
> daughter during their attempt to liberate themselves.

At a time when therapies focus either on the individual or on the family, it is well worth remembering this warning that when taking an adolescent into analysis or psychotherapy, we should also consider the parents' capacities and needs. The price of neglecting this will often be losing our patient.

Three stages of adolescence

Early

Here, we come across a child who finds his or her body changing in many different ways: size, hair distribution, voice pitch in the male, growing sexual organs and so on. A girl needs to learn how to cope with her periods, much as a boy has to adapt to his capacity to ejaculate. Finding her breasts developing in size can be a source of conflict for a girl, as can the boy's eventual comparisons of his penis with those of other boys and men. Soon they discover that not only are other youngsters attracted to them, but also they experience feelings of attraction and/or revulsion towards others around them, which can be accompanied by body sensations they have to make sense of, perhaps even before they learn to label these as "sexual".

When does this process of change begin? Most authors quote the age of 12 years as marking the beginning of adolescence, but there is immense variation in different individuals and populations that has to be taken into account. Furthermore, the individual's notions of where his development stands may be quite different from what those around him assume to be the case. Even as we think of "delayed" or "premature" adolescence, it is important to explore the adolescent's experiences of his own position. His ability or otherwise to voice his views about the changes taking place in his body and the way in which the world now treats him will enable us to reach an understanding of his unconscious relationships to himself and to his objects. This is part of any good therapy, but on another level, we should remember that during these early (teen or pre-teen) years, the child/adolescent is likely to arouse sympathy and warmth whenever he or she voices discomfort, anxiety or fear, or behaves in ways that are considered to depart from the "ordinary" and move towards the pathological range of reactions. As they grow older, this sympathy gives way to more complex responses emanating from their environment. If this interest/ sympathy is welcome, the early adolescent is also likely to experience at times varying degrees of shame when coming in contact with family and strangers, since conscious and unconscious feelings of strangeness *vis-a-vis* his body are experienced as something "everybody" else feels about him, i.e., not about his body, but about him as an entire person. This is a point to be remembered: to the adolescent, his body is (unconsciously experienced as) his self.

Middle

In English, the expression "teen years" describes the period of change from the "childish" early adolescent to eventual near-adult. These are years when youngsters have to fumble their way through disentangling the values of their earlier life that they wish to continue to adopt from those they want to discard. In other words, to separate parents' principles, beliefs, rules, mores, etc., which have constituted his "education", from what he now discovers himself impelled to adopt on the basis of his new (physical and emotional) capacities and the impact of interactions with his peers. Conceptually, we want to consider his object representations—the result of interactions with parents and other early objects—and how these now influence and are influenced by the adolescent's new experiences with parents and others. If, in early adolescence, the youngster's attempts at self-assertion were seen as a "cute" or a charming kind of awkwardness, similar (from the adolescent's point of view) manifestations of self-confidence may now be taken as acts of rebellion and defiance that gradually give rise to clashes and battles. The parents may accuse youngsters of wanting to dominate them, while youngsters may accuse parents of wanting to squash them and treat them as mere children. An outsider will recognize that these power struggles are, in a sense, inevitable: each party is trying to cope with an unconscious (and sometimes conscious) ambivalence about the disengagement that will enable the adolescent to become independent and self-sufficient. Understandably, this phase acquires extra poignancy in one-parent families: we must not lose sight of the social significance of that parent being left to live on his or her own.

In practice, as long as adolescent and parents go on fighting, the clinician can believe there exists hope of a positive resolution. On the other hand, prognosis is more guarded and pathology is more likely to develop when these roles are reversed (i.e., a parent breaks down and the youngster has to assume the role of caretaker) or when adolescent and/or parent(s) abandon their battles and write each other off. When disengagement/disowning occurs, serious crises can develop. Most times, the adults manage to deal with the resulting feelings of failure and guilt by covering them up with self-justifying anger or contempt. For the adolescent, however, the experience of being written off by one or both parents can be extremely traumatic. Not only does he lose their protection, but most times he will take upon himself the blame for the breakdown of the relationship: the resulting blend of guilt, resentment and despair can lead to destructive relationship patterns that are repeated with increasing erosion of self-esteem and, quite often, danger to life.

But during the middle phase of adolescence, whatever the youngster feels, he or she is still dependent on the parents. In our society, at least, young people will usually be living with parents and relying on them for food, money, schooling, etc. Over the last few decades we have seen a dramatic change in these patterns as the use of drugs and sexual customs that used to characterize the late phase of adolescence are practised by ever younger adolescents. Predictably, parallel changes have affected the structure of the family: unemployment, job shortages, the need for both parents to work, new views on pregnancy, marriage and family obligations, all combine to create a blurring in the transition from middle to late adolescence. From a practical point of view of having to work with an adolescent, we must investigate and take into account not only any possible gap between his emotional and his physiological stage of maturity but also the actual family and community environment in which he lives.

Late

These are the years when adolescents may go to university, find employment, leave home to pair up with one or more peers; or, if they still live at home with their parents, they may become increasingly able to reach a *modus vivendi* in which confrontations occur less frequently than do situations of mutual tolerance and perhaps even amicable togetherness. But, as they find their way to recognizing the various components of their sense of self, adolescents can also experience powerful feelings of isolation. Having left behind the sense of "self-in-the-family" developed up to that point, they may seek the company of peers to achieve a new sense of belonging. In a sense this is a normal process, but we should differentiate between the youngster who is reasonably self-sufficient and seeks others of the same age out of a desire to socialize from another who needs company to escape from loneliness. Some adolescents learn to disguise their sense of isolation through various stratagems, but in fact this is a type of depression and when it sets in the adolescent can feel abandoned and reach a degree of despair that often leads to self-destructive behaviour. Another common solution for such crises is the pairing up with someone who is felt to be able to offer the longed for protection, company and love . This often takes the appearance of sexual behaviour and, indeed, this is how the adolescent will usually present it, but we must remember the possibility that sex is being used as an attempt to deal with a much wider and deeper sense of estrangement from the self and the objects that had represented sources of emotional security.

Later

Most societies will consider the 18-year-old to be a virtual adult. though the celebrations for the twenty-first birthday represent a more realistic appraisal of a person's degree of maturity. Nevertheless, we all meet people older than this who appear to be struggling with the conflicts we normally associate with adolescence. Astor (1988) coined the expression "adolescent state of mind" to describe such individuals, which is more accurate than simply saying they are "emotionally immature". Many years earlier, Bernfeld (1923) described a specific kind of male adolescent, "the protracted type", who retains adolescent characteristics well beyond the usual chronological boundaries and shows "tendencies toward productivity whether artistic, literary or scientific and a strong bend toward idealistic aims and spiritual values".

Conceptualizing findings

Within a psychoanalytic framework, all schools appear to agree that adolescence represents a developmental stage where the person moves from dependence on the parents to the independence that characterizes adulthood. This progression has been juxtaposed to the similar developmental process that leads the infant to grow from birth to latency: it follows from this that adolescence is seen as a "second chance" in the pursuit of self-sufficiency and independence. The basic premise for this formulation is the theory of unconscious mental representations of the child's objects; psychoanalysis sees:

> adult behaviour ... as an elaboration or evolution of infantile behaviour, and complex "higher" forms of behaviour can be interpreted as elaborations of simple, primitive behaviour patterns and drives. [Rycroft 1968]

It is this assumption that underlies the interpretation of adolescents' behaviour as resulting from their relationship to their "early objects". But recognizing in an adolescent's behaviour and account the features that justify this interpretation should not blind us to the fact that the circumstances of the adolescent's life are dramatically different from those present in early childhood. When a 12-year-old is described as behaving like a toddler, this signifies an emotional regression, which may well indicate the presence of some pathology. Even if we interpret our patient's feelings and behaviour along the lines of his earliest object relationships, we must still note how he experiences life with his actual, present parents. It is this that helps us to evaluate his capacity to distinguish between the reality of their present attributes from the images of the parents that he has internalized in his earlier years. Understanding the meaning of a patient's feelings, words and behaviour should not preclude the assessment of his capacity to perceive the reality of the world in which he lives.

Ideally, one should, in my view, choose a body of theory *after* one has gained some clinical experience. In practice, theories are learnt from lectures and books *before* approaching patients and this cannot but lead to one's experiences being interpreted already within that body of theory one has learnt to follow. Although clinical work can never be theory free, it is useful to remember that theories were constructed in order to make sense of clinical findings. This should help us to scrutinize various theories until we find the one(s) that best makes sense for us of our observations. Instinct theory, object relations, attachment, Kleinian or ego psychology are not necessarily mutually exclusive theoretical frameworks and they should be used with the main objective of helping us to understand and formulate what we observe. When conveying our findings to others it becomes important to make sure that our formulations can be understood. I believe, however, that if we have reached a good understanding of the patient, our formulations are likely to be coherent and comprehensible (whether they command agreement or not!), whatever theoretical framework we adopt.

Meeting the patient

There has been a growth of walk-in services for adolescents and these will always be sought by the youngster him/herself.

Administrative procedures vary from centre to centre, but the therapist is bound to see the patient on his or her own for their initial meeting. When private therapists receive the referral of an adolescent by letter or any other means, they have to decide *whom* they will meet first. Clearly, before learning the details of a case, there is no way of guessing which technical approach will bring the best results and therapists can only follow their preferred method of working. Personally, whatever the age of the adolescent, I prefer to meet initially the youngster and both parents, since this helps all of us to know exactly why and how we are proposing to proceed. A useful (for me) rule of thumb is that the younger the adolescent, the more important it is to see him together with the parents. Late adolescents, on the whole, prefer to be seen alone and, usually, their parents are quite happy to see the therapist also on their own. I have found that it is quite useful for therapists to make it explicit to the adolescent and to both parents that they reserve the right to call for joint interviews if they believe this is necessary. Many analysts choose to refer one or both parents to another colleague, so that they can restrict their involvement to the individual work with the adolescent. In such cases one should be clear about the rationale for this approach and I believe it must be discussed carefully with the parent(s). Often enough, the first contact with the analyst comes from parents who request an appointment and explicitly ask to meet the analyst in the absence of the adolescent. I am usually willing to accept this, though I make a point of informing them of my usual way of working as this helps us to discuss their request, rather than my having to simply accept or deny the parents' wishes.

In some instances the adolescent does not wish the parents to be seen. This poses a more difficult problem. I always agree to see the adolescent on his or her own, in the first instance, but before or during the interview I insist that I should see the parents—preferably together with the adolescent. Of course, confidentiality has to be preserved, but there are a number of issues (e.g. fees) that have to be discussed with the parents and, apart from any practical considerations, it is always useful to learn from each parent how they see their child's problems. If, during the meeting with the adolescent, it becomes clear that there are problems (e.g. drugs, pregnancy) that may require informing the parents or the family doctor, this should, I think, be discussed in detail with the adolescent. Occasionally, it can happen that the adolescent forbids the consultant to contact anyone else: the consultant may decide that, whatever dangers he perceives in the adolescent's situation, he will agree to that request, but it is then extremely important that he make careful and detailed notes about this. Ideally, such a decision should be discussed with a colleague, but this is not always possible, which makes it imperative that the consultant should write down his arguments for reaching this conclusion. Delicate and painful issues of confidentiality are at stake, but then the analyst is also responsible for the patient's care. Weighing up the pros and cons of stepping out of a strictly analytic posture can be a very difficult problem. The following clinical examples are illustrative.

> A 19-year-old who had been in analysis for nearly two years became involved with drug addicts and I was told of their experiments with various drugs, including heroin. This was an intelligent arid sophisticated youngster, but he lived virtually on his own, with few relations alive. He always attended his sessions punctually, but one day he did not turn up. I telephoned him and when I had no reply, I contacted the police. They gained entrance to the flat and found the patient in a nearly comatose state. He recovered well, but then sent me a letter stating that he could no longer trust me. I wrote to him explaining my decision and I tried to persuade him to return and discuss the situation. He refused. A few weeks later one of his relatives contacted me to say that the patient had died of a drug overdose.

> A 20-year-old patient complained of persistent headaches. This was after one year of analysis and all kinds of interpretations had made no impact on the headaches. He consulted the health services of his university, who decided this was a psychogenic complaint. As the headaches continued unabated, I insisted on a second opinion. The physician who saw the patient immediately asked for various tests and found a brain tumour. The patient was operated upon, but died after a few days.

The first meeting must make the adolescent feel that here is a professional who is able, willing and, in fact, determined to give him or her the opportunity of being heard and, hopefully, understood. This is not an easy task, since we must assume that the youngster is highly sensitive to how adults react to him as a person and may, for example, resent firmness as much as he may be suspicious of kindness. Perhaps the key attitudes to show are respect and interest, but the atmosphere one generates out of one's experience and personality is equally significant, though more difficult to define. The therapist, however, has to use this first interview to assess the seriousness of the patient's problem. It is not always possible in one session to reach a clear idea of the nature and gravity of what brings the youngster to us, but we must establish whether any urgent issues demand prompt attention or whether we can take our time for an extended diagnostic evaluation of the case.

Over the last few decades, there has been what can only be called a glorification of the notion that the therapist should concentrate on the "here and now" of the meeting with the patient. Whether this is a universally applicable proposition is debatable, but when it is put into practice during an assessment interview, the results can be regrettable. Consultants should have a clear idea of the problem areas they want to explore in conducting their evaluation of each individual patient's needs and this is particularly important when seeing adolescents. When the consultant takes the stance that whatever the patient says and does reflects the "psychic truth" of his or her relationship to the interviewer, he will assume a receptive, non-active, non-probing posture and this may interfere with his capacity to question or challenge the adolescent's communications. An assessment interview places a serious responsibility on the consultant that is quite different from a situation where a patient is being assessed for his suitability for long-term therapy. It is a simple fact that we have no way of deciding when patients are telling us the truth or when they are opting for deception or evasion, but in ongoing therapy this is not such a major difficulty. However, when seeing an adolescent for a diagnostic evaluation, it becomes extremely important for the consultant to voice any suspicions that he is not being allowed to obtain a proper knowledge of the patient's situation.

If we are meeting the adolescent together with his parent(s), we must respect the adolescent's right to privacy and it is, therefore, useful to stress that he or she should feel free not to answer any questions we ask (this right applies to the parents as well!). We can add that there may be things he would prefer to tell us in private and that we intend to see him on his own in due course. It is impossible to cover all eventualities to be explored in an initial assessment, but two main indications of serious pathology should be mentioned: psychosis and self-destructive behaviour. Some youngsters may volunteer sufficient information for us to recognize the presence of one of these, but usually we have to formulate appropriate questions in order to elicit pointers for either diagnosis. Self-cutting, eating compulsions, suicidal impulses, use of drugs, involvement with dangerous company or activities, and perverse or risk-taking sexual practices are behaviours that will usually only be revealed in private, away from the parents' presence. Nevertheless, if a reference to any of these activities emerges in front of the parents, it is important to explore the attitudes (overt and covert) of each parent (a) to what their child has said and (b) to the particular subject itself, e.g. what each parent thinks of body weight, use of marijuana or other drugs, etc. I am not suggesting that one should go through a questionnaire on antisocial behaviours. I have in mind situations where adolescents make a reference to some "objectionable" activity and one or both parents dismiss this as, say, the youngster trying to call attention on him/herself or pretending they are a more active member of their crowd than they (the parents) "know them to be". For the consultant to accept such an assertion without comment may appear to be his choosing which of them he believes—in other words, a kind of taking sides. It is preferable to suggest they leave out, at least for the moment, whether the adolescent's claim is fact or fiction and request each parent to explain his or her attitude to that particular behaviour. If we have, for example, an adolescent who feels tormented by a compulsion to experiment with drugs and we find the parents speaking about drugs in some dismissive, contemptuous way ("Oh, today's kids are determined to experiment with just about anything! It's a phase they all go through!"), this will give us a live demonstration of why the adolescent feels unprotected, as if some insurmountable barrier existed between him and his parent(s).

Here is a relevant clinical example,

A depressed 15-year-old told me of going to boarding school because his "parents wanted to get rid of [him]" and gave me examples of his friends avoiding him. On the whole, he said, he felt "bored" and I suggested he meant "hopeless". When I met him with his parents, he restricted his account to his troubles with various teachers. When he finally managed to voice his sense of isolation and depression, his father snapped:

"Oh! He doesn't mean it! He just needs to discover a passion for some subject! School is boring, I never liked it, either! In the 60s, everyone was having sex with everyone, I didn't like it, so it's no surprise he doesn't want to mix with anyone!"

As the discussion proceeded, it became clear that the boy's father felt quite incapable of any proximity with the boy, choosing instead to work very long hours. Subsequent regular individual therapy brought forward the boy's difficulties in developing his gender identity.

It can happen that a parent tries to use the consulting-room environment to extract a confession from their child. The consultant has to be sensitive to the adolescent's feelings: some youngsters may welcome the opportunity to get across to their parents what they have been struggling with, but others may choose to limit what they want to say. In such situations, I usually point out that we are not in a courtroom and I try to get everyone to concentrate on the feelings that influence their living together, rather than on an apparent pursuit of "the entire truth". We must remember that, whatever their unconscious motivations, most parents view inter-views as an opportunity to obtain guidance as to how best to help their child. Even if we have already formed an opinion about the adolescent's problems, any advice to the parents must take into account how each parent perceives their child's present situation. We have to evaluate the extent to which they can distinguish between their own feelings, beliefs and prejudices and those of the adolescent's. This is not a question of exploring moral views (very often, of course, the consultant will be asked what he thinks, e.g. of the use of cannabis; one father demanded that I confirm his view that coffee was a damaging drink in view of its high caffeine content), but rather an attempt to evaluate the capacity of each parent for perceiving and experiencing the adolescent as a separate human being and not simply a part of themselves. This is a vital element in the assessment of the framework against which we have to make sense of the adolescent's behaviour, especially if we consider that the parents' level of object relationships will have affected the whole of the adolescent's emotional development. The parents should not, therefore, be seen only as "sources of informa-tion" about the adolescent: their personal and marital history, characteristics and needs should be explored with due attention. I raise this issue by turning to each parent after the adolescent has given me his picture of "the problems" and the parents have also voiced their interpretation of these problems. I ask them to give me some idea of their own individual backgrounds, "so that I can understand his problem within some kind of context". Usually, parents smile, puzzled and embarrassed, but however reluctant they purport to be, they tend to recognize the importance of seeing their son not just as "another problem child", but as a member of their family and part of their past and present lives.

My emphasis on assessing the capacities of each parent follows from the assumption that, whatever theories we employ in terms of the causation of mental/emotional problems, it is an indis-putable fact that the adolescent and the parents live together and they influence each other in multiple, helpful and harmful, ways. A proper evaluation of the adolescent's needs must establish how each parent will react to any changes in his behaviour: whatever conclusions we come to will influence our choice of treatment to recommend.

Psychosis

A psychotic illness that has progressed to the point where the patient has lost insight into the abnormality of his experiences is quite easy to recognize and the referrer and both parents will be able to notice this is the case. A more difficult diagnostic challenge is posed when the adolescent reports, with considerable fear and anxiety, experiences that *feel* real even if *known* to be abnormal, or when he recounts experiences that are clearly illogical and yet that he appears to consider normal. Such psychotic ideation can be no more than the temporary result of complex individual and/or family dynamics (or, at times, the result of the use of drugs) but it can also indicate the initial stages of a psychotic illness. Depending on the age of the patient, the manner in which he responds to his psychotic perceptions (some adolescents can become agitated and threaten to harm themselves or others), and the circumstances of home life, it may be necessary to consider admission to hospital or referral to a psychiatrist, who may decide to put the patient on medication. If the adolescent appears to retain sufficient insight into his misperceptions and demonstrates a good capacity to cope with upsurges of anxiety, then urgent and intensive therapy can be embarked upon—but in such a case it is vital to ensure that the parents feel supported effectively in their task of looking after the adolescent. In some cases, our assessment may reveal that one or both parents are intimately involved in the patient's life (one mother would sit for hours late into the night discussing with her son his anxieties and his feelings about his psychotherapy session earlier in the day). It is then important to establish (1) to what extent the parent's psychopathology makes it difficult for him or her to tolerate the adolescent becoming involved/dependent on the therapist, and (2) whether the patient's needs are perhaps not sufficiently met by the therapy sessions. However difficult it is for the therapist to disentangle these two possibilities, it is important that he evaluate this "with care and determination, to avoid the danger of the therapy being terminated without him being consulted. If the parent(s) find it difficult to cope with their situation, it is useful to have a working relationship with colleagues who can undertake a supportive role in the therapeutic programme by seeing the parent(s) and helping them to co-operate with the adolescent's treatment.

Self-damaging behaviour

This presents a different diagnostic challenge. Parents are rarely aware of their child's self-damaging behaviour. If a youngster allows his parents to know that he feels depressed and/or suicidal, we must note the positive element of his belief that others can help him. Sadly, most self-destructive behaviour is carried out in private, as part of a conviction of being someone not worth helping or of not trusting the world to wish or be able to help. Isolation, loneliness and hopelessness are the key features in these situations. The youngster feels fear, shame, self-loathing and despair, but when he comes to see us, we have to search for any remaining flicker of hope, which, when present, may be expressed in terms of a challenge as to what motivates our involvement—a "what is it to you?" attitude.

The distinction usually drawn between the patient who comes to see us of his own volition or is forced to come to see us can be, in practice, misleading. It is better to assume (even if we are eventually proved wrong!) that only in exceptional circumstances can an adolescent patient be forced to see a professional. If he is there with us, this may well mean that some minimal degree of ambivalence is still lurking somewhere in his mind. The challenge here is how to convey to him that we have picked up his ambivalence without making him feel exposed; it is a question of finding a way to help him to attend again, even it appears to be, as it were, on his terms. We may come to recognize that no regular treatment is possible at this point and that we have to be content to plant a seed in his mind that might enable him to return to us at some later point.

Adolescents who are cutting themselves or exposing themselves to life-threatening situations (e.g. drugs, unprotected sex, dangerous company) can arouse considerable anxiety in the consultant and yet, regrettably, many of these patients are reluctant to accept offers of therapy. These are situations where the consultant can only rely on his intuition and empathy: some patients can respond positively to a blunt confrontative statement of the kind "you are really in a mess and I think you'd better admit it", while others may respond better to a "gentle" argument leading them to acknowledge the despair and loss of hope underlying their behaviour. But the consultant must not forget that an adolescent involved in risk-taking activities is struggling with very low self-esteem; he longs for an outsider's proof that he can be valued, wanted and loved. And yet, any word or gesture that he perceives as promising to give him such help can arouse (1) a suspicion that the therapist is being moved by his own feelings and needs, rather than recognizing that he, the patient, is nothing like the person the therapist imagines him to be, (2) guilt that he is accepting help from a stranger, rather than turning to his parents, friends or relations, and (3) terror that he may eventually disappoint this stranger who wants to help him. This situation, where the consultant is in constant danger of having his motives questioned, creates an experience of considerable self-consciousness. In practice, the therapist is on guard, lest he be suddenly accused of holding prejudices or harbouring some messianic needs, either of which are likely to be felt like attacks on the person of the therapist, rather than comments about his professional motivations. These challenges result from the adolescent projecting on to the therapist the opposite poles of his self- and object-representations: total love and total condemnation towards someone who is seen, at the same time, as a loved and a despicable person. Only slow and consistent work on this dynamic configuration may lead the patient to take stock of his view of himself and the world around him—but this requires that the adolescent should embark upon and stay in therapy.

Eating problems present a different kind of challenge. Even if they have become a common feature of middle-class occidental society, they quite often constitute the presenting symptom of severe underlying pathology. It is prudent to recognize all variations of eating problems as part of self-damaging pathology, but, particularly in the case of anorexia nervosa, we have to bear in mind the physical condition of the patient. These are patients who require the therapist to have close links with a medical colleague who can supervise the condition of the patient's metabolism. The same precaution applies to those patients who are referred for help with their emotional problems, but who are under medical care for conditions such as diabetes, asthma, epilepsy, rheumatic diseases, coeliac disease, etc. Many of these patients experience their illnesses as an attack by their bodies on their self: the body is seen as an enemy, a persecutor that the youngster wants to defy and dominate. At times they will stop taking the drugs or following the diets required to keep their illness under control and this forces us to consider them as involved with self-destructive behaviour. During adolescence, these psychosomatic problems become telescoped with issues of gender identity and the impossibility of achieving total independence and "normality", since the illness is seen to inflict on the adolescent the need to depend on doctors and drugs.

A clinical example here is of a 16-year-old girl who was referred because of "eating problems".

Both the patient and her parents spoke at great length about diets, weight and multiple clashes over these issues. There was no doubt that the young woman was unhappy and depressed. They were quite happy to accept the offer of individual psychotherapy to help the patient with her problems. But detailed questioning about the girl's physical development had brought out the information that she had still not had any periods. The family accepted a referral to a paediatric endocrinologist and this revealed that the patient had a serious congenital malformation of her ovaries. Psychotherapy was embarked upon, but appropriate medication was also given.

All authors agree on the importance of sexuality for the adolescent, but we must not forget that often adolescents will use sexual feelings and activities as a means of expressing anxieties that belong to other areas of their sense of self in the world. The danger for the consultant or therapist is to neglect these deeper anxieties (that may involve feelings about living and dying) and focus on sex in a manner that the youngster may interpret (1) as a blindness to other anxieties or (2) as the result of a moralistic attitude that he probably experiences from his parents and also from his own conscience. Either way, the adolescent will feel disappointed and helpless.

Frequency of sessions

The therapist makes life easier for himself if he only works under one fixed scheme of sessions. If, however, he varies the frequency with which he sees his patients depending on the severity of their pathology, he has to develop and follow his diagnostic criteria for such decisions—no easy task. Hopefully, the consultant should be able to decide what he considers *the ideal* treatment he would recommend for that particular patient. Once he puts this forward, he has to decide whether he is prepared to accept some counter-proposal from the patient and/or parents or whether he will refuse to take responsibility for the patient unless his recommendation is accepted. There is no end of (conscious and unconscious) reasons why patient and/or parents will dispute the consultant's advice, but at the end of the day it is the consultant who has the final word about his further involvement in the case. I believe each practitioner is entitled (expected, in fact) to know the conditions under which he works at his best and if this involves the number of sessions he gives each patient, so be it. But he should make this reason explicit, rather than imply that such conditions are being put forward for the benefit of the patient.

Don Campbell (1992) reviewed the literature on the criteria utilized by various analysts to establish the frequency of sessions in analytic work with adolescents. Most papers published in the psychoanalytic world focus on the "suitability for psychoanalysis", which is not necessarily synonymous with determining which helping programme best applies to a particular patient. Campbell's survey is written with sensitivity and is clearly based on wide experience of work in different settings, which brings the advantage of not stemming exclusively from clinical work with children of families who want and can support (financially and emotionally) their child's visits to a private professional. He quotes Eglé Laufer's (1991) argument that adolescents in danger of a breakdown or who present a tendency to serious acting out should be seen in full psychoanalysis; this view is supported by Yorke (1965). In contrast to these authors, Berman (1971) lists "psychosis, borderline states, severe delinquency, hypochondriacal complaints, exclusive cathexis of peers and hostile or seductive involvement with parents, loss of control or severely rigid control of impulses" as contra-indications to psychoanalysis. Clearly, issues of diagnostic definition are involved here, but it is far more difficult to establish the role of the consultant's personal style and bias on the final choice of treatment.

Discussions about the frequency of sessions involve complex and conflicting arguments over what are effective and, perhaps, legitimate ways of helping a patient with emotional and behavioural problems. The nature of the work we practise does not allow us to submit the same patient, at the same point of his life, to two different forms of treatment. We cannot, therefore, but accept the consequences of the fact that, with each particular patient, we put into practice the approach we believe to be the best we can offer him. This makes for considerable difficulties when it comes to comparing views expressed by professionals who follow different theoretical and technical schools. Campbell's paper is exceptional in his description of how he does his best to adapt his idea of what the adolescent would *ideally* need to what the adolescent is prepared/able to accept (*op. cit.*, p. 110). This is an approach with which I strongly agree. If the analyst presents himself from a standpoint of knowledge, sympathy and seriousness, his flexibility, his willing-ness to mould his views to the reality of the patient's abilities cannot but reassure the adolescent (or a patient of any age) that here is someone who is sufficiently interested and cares for him enough to allow him to establish his own timing in developing a relation-ship of trust that may bring him some eventual benefit. This is not the same as saying that we allow the patient to dictate the number of sessions we are to have, but rather that a serious discussion can be held about this, where patient and analyst express and justify their viewpoints until a compromise can be reached to the satisfac-tion of both.

It should be noted that an adolescent who promptly and eagerly accepts the assessor's recommendation may be giving an early warning of an all-or-nothing type of attachment, which is based on faith and a very limited capacity for reality testing: just as quickly as he can (apparently) surrender into compliance, so can he shift to paranoid anxieties and take flight without warning. This should be recognized as a psychotic transference in a patient who cannot develop a working alliance with the therapist. I would agree with Campbell, Laufer and Yorke that an adolescent who presents psychotic anxieties and shows poor capacity for self-control by endangering his life through serious acting out should be seen as many times per week as possible. Whether this comes to be five or four or any other number of sessions each week, the objective is to endeavour to help the adolescent to bring his pathological ideation, wishes and impulses into the treatment room.

But the success or failure of any contract for therapy with a disturbed adolescent depends on too many factors and I have tried to discuss some of these. In practice, to my mind, working with adolescents demands flexibility and a preparedness to be alert not only to fluctuations in the therapeutic relationship, but also to other factors that may be playing a part in the young-ster's life. Helping the parents or a school, when the adolescent allows us to do so, can be of great importance in securing the continuation of the one-to-one work with an adolescent. If, however, we are seeing a late adolescent who does not allow us to contact anyone other than himself, this can create situations of great anxiety for the analyst: he cannot but try to work through these with the patient.

Technique

Much has been written about the features that characterize a psycho-analytic treatment and in what way psychotherapy should be conducted. Now we speak of psychoanalytic psychotherapy and this appears to signify a treatment in which the patient is seen for fewer than four or five sessions each week but the therapist conducts his therapy as if he was seeing his patient four or five times per week. When seeing adolescents only once or twice a week, the therapist is likely to go through painful moments, since these are patients who experience peaks of anxiety and impulsiveness precisely at a time of life where a capacity for self-control is one of their main problems. Similar crises can occur even when the adolescent is being seen five times per week, but when sessions are less frequent the therapist is likely to feel more anxious, e.g. by blaming himself for taking on that patient under such "misguided" conditions. Analysts and therapists, like all members of the helping professions, are entitled to reassess their findings. As treatment progresses, the therapist may decide that his patient requires more or less frequent sessions than those being followed; when this happens, he should make it the subject of open discussion. This reassessment is different from the ordinary, frequent occurrence of experiencing sudden, intense, powerful feelings when seeing an adolescent in crisis.

When a therapist is seeing an adolescent once or twice per week, it can happen that the youngster describes situations and feelings which make the therapist experience intense feelings that lead him to want to argue, advise or admonish. Some will say that this is a counter-transference response: the therapist is identifying himself with the patient's unconscious image of a parental figure who has let him down and now tries to make up for this by blaming the adolescent for doing something wrong. This formulation may leave out the possibility that the therapist might hold a belief that the "truly helpful" way of helping a patient is by giving him the ideal effective therapy of four- or five times-per-week analysis. Both possibilities must be seriously considered. When we manage to separate out the patient's anxieties from the therapist's value systems, we can interpret the adolescent's material more correctly—in this case, irrespective of the frequency of sessions that has been decided upon. A disturbed adolescent in pain arouses very powerful feelings in us, but it is always prudent to consider that a proportion of these feelings originate in us. Particularly during the phase where a therapist is learning to work with adolescents, it is important that he scrutinize his feelings carefully before deciding that they stem from the patient's projections. This advice is based on my conviction that however moved we may be by the distress of an adult patient, this cannot compare with the intensity of feelings we experience when trying to help a child or an adolescent. And there is the additional factor that the younger the therapist, the more prone will he be to imagine himself in the position of the youngster. Only if he analyses his feelings with great care will he be able to recognize what belongs to the patient and what is part of his own professional development. An automatic counter-transference interpretation may be a convenient short-circuit that could spoil a valuable learning opportunity.

A frequent argument in work with adolescents refers to the type of interventions that the therapist/analyst is supposed to make. There are analysts who demand that only transference interpretations should be used. but these tend to be the analysts who make the same prescription for the analyses of children and of adults. Other analysts are prepared to accept that work with children involves other interventions than solely transference interpretations. When it comes to adolescents. I think one experiences difficulties that are linked to their developmental stage: they do not play with toys or drawings as younger children do and they do not see the therapist as strictly a professional as adults will do. Because of their conscious and unconscious struggles to disengage from their parental figures, and because of their changing views of language as a means of communication, adolescents will one minute treat the therapist as a "mate" or older friend who can understand what they feel without their having to try too hard to convey it to him, and the next minute as another parental figure who wants to criticize, preach, indoctrinate and dominate them. A perfectly correct transference interpretation can, sometimes, be experienced as a complaint or a seductive move. In other words, some adolescents can understand words as signifying shared symbols, much as they can suddenly take words quite literally. Personally, I try to formulate my interventions as if they were part of a dialogue: not between equals, but aiming to make the adolescent feel that it is *his* view that I am interested in. Instead of putting forward a statement purporting my idea about his unconscious feelings, I would invite/provoke him to explain or reconsider a statement of his that might lead him to arrive at the same interpretation I might have given myself.

For example:

> A 19-year-old young man had amassed a long series of initial successes that were promptly followed by failures. One day, he quoted something I had said two sessions earlier, commenting that he was surprised at being able to remember it. A bit later, he mentioned an older man with whose family he had lived for several years: he felt that the man had given him enormous encouragement in dealing with life. Later, the patient mentioned a friend to whom he was very attached for a long period; he said this was a charismatic figure whose company made him "feel great". When he embarked on another long account of his compulsive attempt at being accepted, clearly without believing he would succeed, I reminded him of his words about those two men and asked whether they represented sources of some special power? He beamed, "Oh, they really made me feel a winner!" I then asked if remembering my words had any particular significance and he laughed, "I guess it reminded me of them . . . ".

There is no doubt that it is quite difficult to make an adolescent engage in long-term therapy, but provided this is what the analyst believes the youngster needs, he can only treat each meeting as if there was to be a next one at the previously arranged time. The adolescent is, by definition, examining the analyst's every word and move for cues to gauge how he sees him. The closer the analyst sticks to his professional stance and shows his interest in the fact that the patient has come to see him, the better the prospect that the patient will also stop and consider the meaning of his presence in that room. With luck, he will eventually recognize that his attendance signifies that he has allowed an element of doubt to seep into his previous conviction that he and his world were hopelessly lost. Some adolescents take flight at this point, but some decide to look further into what they have made of their lives.

References

Anderson, R., & Dartington, A. (Eds.) (1998). *Facing Out*, Duckworth.

Astor, J. (1988). Adolescent states of mind found in patients of different ages seen in analysis. *Journal of Child Psychotherapy, 14*(1): 67–80.

Herman (1971). Quoted in Sklansky, M. A. (1972). Indications and contraindications for the psychoanalysis of the adolescent. *Journal of the American Psychoanalytic Association, 20*, 134–144.

Bernfeld, S. (1923). Über eine typische Form de mäninlichen Pubertät. *Imago, IX.*

Blos, P. (1967). The second individuation process of adolescence. *Psychoanalytic Study of the Child, 5*(22): 162–186.

Campbell, D. (1992). Introducing a discussion of frequency in child and adolescent analysis. *Psychoanalysis in Europe, 38*, 105–113.

Erikson, E. (1965). *Childhood and Society,* Hogarth.

Freud, A. (1958). Adolescence. *Psychoanalytic Study of the Child, 8*: 255–278.

Harris, M. (1965). Depression and the depressive position in an adolescent boy. *Journal of Child Psychotherapy, 1*(3): 33–40.

Jones, E. (1922). Some problems of adolescence. In: *Papers on Psycho-Analysis,* Baillière, Tyndall & Cox. [Reprinted in *Collected Papers,* Maresfield, 1948.]

Laufer, E. (1991). Quoted (personal communication) in Campbell, D. (1992) *op. cit.*

Laufer, M. (1976). The central masturbation fantasy, the final sexual organisation and adolescence. *Psychoanalytic Study of the Child, 31*: 297–316.

Laufer, M. (1978). The nature of adolescent pathology and the psychoanalytic process. *Psychoanalytic Study of the Child, 33*: 307–322.

Mahler, M. (1963). Thoughts about development and individuation. *Psychoanalytic Study of the Child, 18*: 307–324.

Rycroft, C. (1968). *A Critical Dictionary of Psychoanalysis,* (1977 edn), p. 34. Penguin.

Segal, H. (1964). *Introduction to the Work of M. Klein.* Heinemann.

Spillius, E. (1988). *Melanie Klein Today,* Volume 2, *Mainly Practice,* pp. 158–167. London: Routledge.

Winnicott, D. W. (1961a). Adolescence: struggling through the doldrums. In: *The Family and Individual Development.* London: Karnac, 1989.

Winnicott, D. W. (1961b). Psychoneurosis in childhood. In: *Psychoanalytic Explorations.* London: Karnac, 1989.

Yorke, C. (1965).'Some metapsychological aspects of interpretation. *British Journal of Medical Psychology, 38*: 27–42.

CHAPTER FOUR

Adolescence

Denis Flynn

I n this chapter I shall look at some central psychoanalytic contributions to the understanding of adolescence. I shall outline some theories that I have found useful in my psychoanalytic work with adolescents and give short vignettes as examples of the use of these theories in two specific areas. Firstly, I shall illustrate the continued relevance of Freud's developmental theory and the reworking of early Oedipal relationships from early adolescence onwards. Secondly, I shall look at the development of psychological structures in adolescence, which can lead to specific adolescent states of mind, and I shall illustrate how the adolescent's use of their mind and sense of their body can be affected in severe disturbances.

I shall define adolescence, understood psychoanalytically, as a developmental process in which the boy or girl, or young man or woman, develop new sexual and aggressive powers, including a powerful and sexual body, as they rework Oedipal relationships in the light of new tasks in life. Young people acquire a new sense of themselves and their physical, mental and emotional capacity, including a sense of their individuality and their personal value. If very severe disturbance takes hold of the adolescent during this developmental process, then the entire process will be affected, and may even be halted.

Adolescence is normally a time of change, of unpredictable and powerful reactions and responses, with the loss of childhood and movement towards adulthood. It is a time when there is a new awareness of the body, a new sense of the personal, experiences of new impulses, an increased awareness of inner feelings and an increased capacity for reflection. There is a changing relationship to groups, to other people including parents and relatives, to authority figures and institutional structures, and a wider sense of society. A normal transition through adolescence involves some measure of disturbance, both of inner feelings and attitudes within oneself, and also in relation to others. These changes occur in adolescence as part of a process of detachment from the parents and the family, and, as with earlier detachment processes in infancy, are accompanied by equally major changes in awareness of the emotional states of others (Stern 1985) and involve alternating periods of integration and lack of integration. Sometimes the adolescent appears static, behind a wall of powerful resistances or defences, and sometimes he or she surges forwards in what seems a haphazard and contradictory way. In adolescence, change can occur at any time.

Disturbance in adolescence can be such that it can be hard to give adolescents sufficient thought and attention. It is not uncommon for parents to wish that adolescence itself would just go away. Shakespeare wrote in *The Winter's Tale* (III.iii.59–63) (quoted in Copley 1993, pp. 100–101):

> I would there were no age between ten and three-and-twenty, or that youth would sleep out the rest; for there is nothing in the between but getting wenches with child, wronging the ancientry, stealing, fighting.

Even Winnicott (1963) seemed to be saying this:

> There is only one cure for adolescence and that is the passage of time and the passing on of the adolescent into the adult state.

Winnicott was saying something much more subtle though, that each individual needs to experience their own adolescence, and live through it, for no outsiders can cure an individual's problems in adolescence.

Our psychoanalytic understanding of adolescence has only really moved forward in the last 50 years. Freud, in his "Three essays on the theory of sexuality" (1905) and elsewhere, wrote of the changes that occur at puberty, specifically noting the reworking of infantile conflicts after major biological changes. There are just six references to "adolescence" in the Index of Freud's work, which refer not so much to his specific psychoanalytic theories of changes at puberty, but to what he called a wider, more generally understood "normal process of adolescence" (Freud, 1893, pp. 125–34), which he never explained or defined. Before Freud, adolescence had a special significance because it was seen as the time when sexual life began. With Freud's introduction of his theory of infantile sexuality, shifting the beginning of sexual life to a period long before adolescence, one could well ask was adolescence itself demoted?

Overall, in Freud's writing, there is little mention of what we would now regard as essential parts of adolescence: emotional growth, major restructuring of the personality and, particularly, adolescent states of mind. Aichhorn (1931) wrote of work with adolescents in residential settings (cf. Freud's 1925 review), and there was some work by the early child psychoanalysts. But Anna Freud herself, in 1936, described adolescence as a "neglected period". It was only after the Second World War, with widespread changes in society, that adolescence became widely recognized as a phenomenon in itself, worthy of study. Not surprisingly, some of the most enduring and expressive literature about adolescence dates from this time, notably Salinger's *The Catcher in the Rye* (1945–1946), and Steinbeck's *East of Eden* (1952). There were also many films about adolescence made at this time and a recognizable culture of adolescence began to develop.

Despite this, our psychoanalytic understanding of adolescence is still based in Freud's developmental model set out in "Three essays on the theory of sexuality". Accordingly, psychological changes at puberty are based on, and derive their power from, physical (i.e. biological) changes that alter and re-evoke the already powerful but by now largely dormant infantile sexuality, which produces changes that "give infantile sexual life its final, normal shape" (*ibid.*, p. 207). There is at this time a convergence of the affectionate current [i.e. the emotional residue of infantile sexuality that still has an open existence, on condition an inhibition is interposed between the infantile sexuality and its natural goal (cf. Jones, 1922, p. 397)], and the sensual current (the fully developed genital sexual feelings) under the primacy of genital feelings.

Freud's views about changes in puberty are consistent with his views on infancy and latency, in that he thought problems occurred in puberty because of "pathological disorders of sexual life", which become manifest as inhibitions in development, for example in a fixation on the pregenital stages, and especially because of unresolved, early and unconscious incestuous phantasies. He saw phallic identifications and castration anxiety as occurring in this way. Puberty brings a search for a new sexual object, normally of the opposite sex. Changes of object choice in puberty do not occur clearly or straight away, and there are periods of trial action where adolescents indulge in phantasies and live in a world of ideas, delaying any action on the basis of their object choices or trying a same-sex object choice before someone of the opposite sex. The changes in libidinal object and aim at puberty involve a progressive development of infantile Oedipal relationships, and the changes protect individuals and society against incest. There is normally a loosening of the connection with the family, both from the incestuous object and phantasies towards the mother or father, and from parental authority. The life force driving these powerful sexual, emotional and relationship changes is the libido, which for Freud is a positive force that moves out from the ego towards objects, creating emotional connections to things and to other people, and then back again into the ego. Problems therefore occur when there is a lack of libido, or there is a disturbance by a recurrence of aspects of infantile sexuality. The libido stored within the ego is described as "narcissistic libido", and for Freud is the source of deeper psychotic disturbance (1905, p. 218). In the simplified diagram below—ego libido and object libido—one can see, in terms of opposite poles of a flow, the way in which deeper narcissistic disturbance and the capacity for contact with external objects and reality correspond, and are related, to each other.

Anna Freud reframed this theory of changes at puberty within Freud's structural theory (1923) of id, ego and super-ego. She emphasized similarities between the early infant period and puberty, in that a relatively strong id confronts a relatively weak ego, albeit an ego that in adolescence commands a greater capacity *ego libido* → *some self-worth* → *narcissistic distortion and delusion and loss of connection with the outside world.*

↕

object libido → *connection with outside world* → *loss of sense of self. control of affect, ability to listen.*

(cf. also Freud, 1914, 1923)

for transformation. This allowed her and other Freudian psychoanalysts, notably Erik Erikson (1968, 1977) and Peter Blos (1962, 1970), to see adolescence as a new period characterized by a distinctive adolescent type of experience, with new defences of a primitive nature (such as asceticism and intellectualization) that operate against the intensity of the new id impulses. Anna Freud (1936, pp. 137–138) gave one of the first succinct psychoanalytic descriptions of adolescence, as follows:

> Adolescents are excessively egoistic, regarding themselves as the centre of the universe and the sole object of interest, and yet at no time in later life are they capable of so much self-sacrifice and devotion. They form the most passionate love relations, only to break them off as abruptly as they began them. On the one hand, they throw themselves enthusiastically into the life of the community and, on the other, they have an overpowering longing for solitude. They oscillate between blind submission to some self-chosen leader and defiant rebellion against any and every authority. They are selfish and materially minded and at the same time full of lofty idealism. They are ascetic but suddenly plunge into instinctual indulgence of the most primitive character. At times their behaviour to other people is rough and inconsiderate, yet they themselves are extremely touchy. Their moods veer between light-hearted optimism and the blackest pessimism. Sometimes they will work with indefatigable enthusiasm and at other times they are sluggish and apathetic.

Melanie Klein's early emphasis (1932) is on the intensity of feelings of anxiety in puberty, "a kind of recrudescence of anxiety which is characteristic of small children". Adolescents are seen to be more able to ward off anxiety with a more successfully developed ego, through interests, activities or sports, and at the same time more likely to succumb very quickly to anxiety. Because of this, psychoanalytic treatment must interpret at the immediate point of anxiety or affect in the immediate transference, linking minute signs of anxiety to get in touch with the adolescent's general affective state. Whilst Anna Freud had stressed how, in adolescence as in infancy, the ego is weaker (than in latency or adulthood), Klein stresses the strength of the super-ego in adolescence (and infancy); she writes (*ibid.*, p. 115):

> . . . the superego determines a compulsive instigation of sexual activities, just as it determines a complete suppression of them, that is to say, that anxiety and a sense of guilt reinforce libidinal fixations and heighten libidinal desires.

The same could be said, I think, about aggressive desires and feelings during adolescence—that anxiety and guilt can both increase the aggressive feelings and the acute internal reactions against those feelings. Consequently the adolescent both experiences more negative feelings and hides them more, and readily splits people and things into good and bad. Klein, like Freud, recognized the adolescent's need for action and for the expression of phantasy, and the way in which the adolescent can avoid reality and action by living in a phantasy world. She also recognized how repression of the now highly developed sexual and aggressive affect can, in some adolescents, lead to complete passivity.

I would now like to give some case studies of young adolescents to illustrate the conflicts they were experiencing as they reached puberty. The first concerns the changes occurring in a young girl approaching menarche.

> Fiona was 12, and her parents had divorced when she was three, when her father "became" gay. In many ways a self-possessed girl, she was referred because she cried frequently and was very unhappy. She saw her problem as how to deal with Dad being gay and Mum always being angry with her. As a child she had struggled and searched for reasons why her parents were not together, but at the age of eight she "knew"—her father had a man living with him and there was only one

place to sleep. Fiona said she could only tell her mother she knew when she was 11, "asking her not to shout at her if she said it". [I think that at an infantile level Fiona blamed her mother and experienced anger towards her, even though overt disagreement and disappointment between her parents was denied or played down, and this external blaming was based on Fiona's self-blame and her self-reproach, which were at the root of much of her unhappiness.]

Before her entry into puberty Fiona was desperately sorting out and putting into place her feelings and conflicts about her parents as a couple. There was an intense and driven quality to the whole process, as week by week she changed emotionally and physically in front of me. She struggled with feelings of loss—of friends if she moved house, of her father—and, as she got to know and trust me in the transference, her fear of losing me, related to her underlying feeling of her own lack of worth. She was quick with direct questions, needing to take the initiative, and eager to be able to trust what she found in her work with me. Fiona soon developed a close and intense contact with me, unusual for a girl her age with a male analyst, but I felt that unconsciously I was viewed like a gay Dad, so that some of the inhibitions against seductive closeness were not there. Like other girls, however, there was fear and confusion about orifices and their products, the messes from the anus and the messy expected discharges from her vagina. There were transference connections with early Oedipal attachments to her father, her pre-Oedipal sexuality, and her current knowledge of her father's homosexuality. This was largely unconscious and came out in the transference, for example in the way she recoiled with horror at some sores I developed around my mouth. [This linked, I thought, to unconscious knowledge and confusion about her father's sexuality, and her own oral neediness.] She also expressed horror at some relatives who were married "even though they were very closely related". [In this the perils and the excitement of possible incestuous contact were apparent.]

Her mixed feelings about being a boy or a girl came through. She asked if I had a daughter, wishing, I thought, to become a special girl for me. But she enjoyed, too, being centre stage in the musical as "Bugsy Malone", and partly wanted to be a kind of tomboy. A tumult of feelings about ugliness or prettiness, and her fears of being weak rather than strong, emerged in the week or two before menarche. She talked openly about how her mother had had to have an abortion after an accident, showing her anxiety about her new procreative capacities, and the "accidents" at periods, which she "knew all about", and indicating her fears about her own self-worth. Her anger now emerged, in the transference at me and "the woman outside", and then at her mother and stepfather for being a couple. When I interpreted this she became babyish again. I interpreted this as defensive and indicating her fear of her aggression at her exclusion by the couple.

During the session after her periods began Fiona spoke in terms of colours, exciting roundabouts and slides. She was relieved and became remarkably calm for the remainder of her sessions before she eventually moved house, and therefore finished treatment.

I thought the work she had done on her view of her developing sexuality and her Oedipal relationships, caught up in complex feelings on different levels about her parents, was deeply important in helping her deal with her anxieties during her transition into puberty.

Four young adolescent boys I treated over the same period had quite different patterns of defence (delinquent, phobic, obsessional and psychotic), although the striking similarities in the underlying pathology highlight Freud's central thesis about changes at puberty. In each case there was the problem of a continuously overly close relationship with the mother, based in different ways on incestuous patterns. The beginning of a separate adolescent development was therefore not possible for each boy; similarly, no clear separate sexual aim could emerge, nor could a new identity. After psychotherapy, which focused around unconscious sexual wishes, infantile regressions and conflicts, particularly in relation to the archaic mother, adolescent development could continue. All the boys did well, except for the one who used psychotic defences. I shall briefly outline two cases, those with phobic and obsessional symptoms.

Brian had been school phobic for over a year. He was an only child whose father had died, and he had become increasingly wrapped up in a couple-type relationship with his anxious and fearful mother. In psychotherapy, he developed a close attachment to me as a father substitute, but he also progressively brought out his feelings about his unmourned father and his sense of his own Oedipal triumph. He steered his way into his early adolescent experience very slowly and gradually by reluctantly relinquishing his latency pursuits and preoccupations. These included maddeningly abstruse games and procedures he would devise, and ways of talking and thinking that could be shared with practically no one except his mother, who seemed to be the sole initiate in Brian's one-person cult. Slowly, as his trust towards me grew and he could acknowledge his homosexual transference to his analyst, Brian became able to accept interpretations about his masturbation phantasies, and acknowledge his own masturbation. He could then acknowledge the complex underlying incestuous phantasies affecting his behaviour, including his inability to separate psychically from his mother by exerting subtle emotional control of her, including physical and social over-closeness. He then experienced strong relief at having, and being allowed to have, new and interesting feelings of his own. Brian would react with excitement and bewilderment, like a toddler or small child, at every new experience. In time he got back to school and extended somewhat his social capacities and friendships. Now, several years later, he is finishing a physics degree at university, and interestingly has been able to move away from what was at root a sole preoccupation with his mother's body, to a detailed scientific study of the nature of things (literally "bodies"), a study of external reality.

Colin came from a very troubled family, and had obsessional defences. Colin's brother, two years older, suffered from haemophilia, but he was aggressive and his behaviour was constantly disruptive, leaving the family and the services around them incapacitated. Colin's father was an ineffective man. He had been made redundant from his work and acted as if he had irrevocably retired from life. Colin's mother was perceptive at times, hard working and long suffering. Although she strove to keep the family together, they were nevertheless paralysed. She tended to babify Colin, who was timid, stuttered very badly, and was frightened of any social situation. Although much smaller and slighter in build than his brother, and having a pleasant, non-confrontational way of relating, Colin was stricken with guilt, anxiety and despair that he had somehow caused his brother's life-threatening haemophilia. His brother made accusations that Colin was trying to kill him, and tried to provoke him into fights. Colin's solution was to lower his head and keep a low profile. In his psychotherapy, Colin was continuously preoccupied with obsessional activity, which was orderly and painfully slow. For hours on end he constructed crudely formed Plasticine figures, which he handled and showed with pride. [In evidence was a regression to a pre-Oedipal level of anal fixation, like the toddler at potty training, whose greatest source of pride and satisfaction is to produce and show his own bodily products, and defend and sustain attacks on them.]

In his transference to me, Colin experienced his timidity and fear that I would restrict him, like a limiting mother. He also exhibited identification with a depressed and withdrawn father. Slowly, over a considerable time, through the psychoanalytic work Colin learnt that he was capable of understanding and producing something worthwhile, and that his own thoughts and feelings were valuable, and could be expressed. He began to realize that he could define his own boundaries with his parents and others, more in terms of what others his age might do, rather than in terms of the guilt and fear that racked him persistently. Subsequently this development continued with the help of a small, caring boarding-school, so that now as a young adult Colin is doing well (he is working happily, independently and productively as a care assistant), despite recently experiencing, and weathering, the very aggressive and destructive suicide of his elder brother in his later adolescence.

To return to psychoanalytic theory, I shall now look at some mechanisms that are crucial both to the radical development of personality in adolescence and to the development of particular adolescent states of mind. Melanie Klein's pivotal 1946 paper. "Notes on some schizoid mechanisms", introduced the mechanisms of primitive splitting and projective identification. Klein defined projective identification as the prototype of the aggressive object relationship, representing an anal attack on an object by means of forcing parts of the ego into it in order to take over its contents or control it. Since then, projective identification has acquired a range of meanings and is a cluster concept (Hinshelwood 1991, pp. 179–208). Klein is describing, essentially, processes in early infancy, when projective and introjective mechanisms enable the infant to deal with primitive fears about survival. Extending Klein's view, I think that in adolescence, as in infancy, continuous processes of projection and introjection are also strongly in action, when there is again the need to learn to survive as a more independent individual in a new world. As part of this, internally, continuous processes of splitting and fragmentation of internal and external objects occur, which alter the boundaries of internal and external reality and the shape of the personality in a fundamentally new way. As mentioned earlier, the adolescent becomes aware of, and relates in a new way to, the nature of external objects and their own bodily and emotional states, and begins to know more fully the nature of the emotional states of others (Klein, 1932, 1946; Stern, 1985).

Bion (1962a,b) extends Klein's theory in terms of the value of containment of positive projective identification. This means inducing in the other person a state of mind as a means of communicating their mental state. It is an essential part of containment from early infancy onwards (Hinshelwood, 1991, p. 184). To apply this concept from infancy to adolescence one needs to remember that throughout adolescence, and indeed in any adolescent's day, there are constant shifts backwards and forwards. In understanding the adolescent, one needs to allow both positive and negative projective identification and a process of differentiating between the two. This will mean consenting to experience the feelings and thoughts of the adolescent in their split and fragmented state in order to contain his own state of mind until some pattern of understanding emerges. Over time, adolescents then learn to contain in their mind the thoughts and feelings that lead to progressive splitting and cycles of projection. They then come to feel that their own mind, and body, can contain what's going on, and they build a new structure in their inner (internal) world. Importantly, too, this process teaches the adolescent a fuller sense of personal value, which is based not simply in the Freudian sense on a new sense of their sexual body and worked-through Oedipal relations, but on their capacity to develop, change and contain themselves. This is what lies behind Winnicott's assertion, quoted earlier, that "the only cure for adolescence is the passage of time", for each individual has to have their own experiences and live through their own adolescence. In this process, we become aware, as do adolescents, of the quality of their emotionality and their own changeability as difficult life choices are faced.

Very severe adolescent disturbance accompanied by what Klein and Bion call "excessive projective identification" leads to a continued confusion and distortion of internal and external reality. Such disturbance can be recognized by paying close attention to one's own counter-transference and assessing the quality of the adolescent's projections. It occurs when there is a fundamental hatred of life and emotional knowledge, rather than a love of life and knowing, which the normally disturbed adolescent feels. Severe self-harm, such as cutting, burning and suicide attempts, occurs in adolescents who cannot accept the value of a new sexual body and a new inner self. Body–mind confusions and splits occur at the deepest levels, so that hatred and a wish to kill can be directed at the body in suicide, self- harm or severe perversions, or at the mind through severe drug abuse or deep depressions (Bion, 1957, 1962a,b; Laufer & Laufer, 1984; Rosenfeld, 1987).

Some borderline patients move between normal and very severe disturbance at different times. With this most disturbed group of adolescents, there may be different functions of the personality, an "adolescent function" and a "borderline function" (cf. Bion, 1957, 1963, for his theory of functions; Rosenfeld, 1965), Clinically, it is refreshing when a patient who has been quite borderline, or confused and deluded, becomes disturbing in an ordinary adolescent way! There is a return to what Winnicott would term the playfulness of adolescence, driven by strong, even if often highly disruptive and disturbing, life forces.

Britton's views (1989) on the Oedipus complex serve as a link between Freud's view and the later views of Klein and Bion, as applied here to adolescence. Just as in the depressive position some capacity to tolerate and accept loss of immediate satisfaction is necessary, so in Oedipal relationships it becomes necessary to accept exclusion and restriction by not being part of the parental couple and their sexuality, and hence to be able to take up what Britton calls "the third position". When internalized, this capacity to accept an actual excluded third position enables the individual to have a concept of the external, the other, in terms of his own experience of being an "other". This capacity to accept the other is an essential part of the adolescent's ability to take his place in the world outside, the bigger scheme of things away from parents and family. When this does not happen—when there is, in Britton's terms, "an Oedipal illusion"—the relation to the outside world is disturbed.

Finally, two clinical examples of adolescent girls to illustrate the radical shifts in processes of projection and introjection during adolescence.

Penny, aged 18, continuously showed swings between co-operative and purposeful efforts, and bombastic and destructive behaviour. She has now finished a year's psychoanalytical treatment in an inpatient adolescent unit (a therapeutic community), and is so far managing independently. [For the complexity of the "transference" in such work, cf. Flynn (1998, 1999); Flynn & Day (2000–2001).] Penny was loud, aggressive and uncontained. She was thrown out of everywhere, school and home, and she had been through 30 placements over the previous three years. She drank heavily, used drugs, had casual unsafe sex, and had sunk to living rough on the street in gangs, sometimes thieving and mugging. In her favour, she had developed a strong and ongoing relationship with a persistent social worker and psychiatrist, had managed some outpatient psychoanalytic psychotherapy and some family meetings, and wanted to change. Penny had an over-close and over-involved relationship with her father, who, although very fond of her, would also violently hit her, or impulsively throw her out. She openly hated her mother and was derogatory about her. She denied her parents had a real life as a couple. Penny had had a history of bowel problems and sphincter control as a child, requiring years of intrusive anal procedures. In treatment, as before, she enacted all of this, with angry verbal and occasionally physical attacks on any social boundary.

My feeling at assessment, my counter-transference, was that "something was missing", although I could not put my finger on exactly what it was. Through months of struggle with her, dealing with angry projections that dismantled or blew apart achievements in terms of understanding or containment of feelings by other patients, or us ourselves, and distorted introjections of what she perceived the treatment was doing to her ("messing her up"), this question of "what was missing?" remained with me. I thought she had communicated something to me, which I had to hold and work with. At times I wondered if it was some hidden incestuous sexual abuse, but over time I discounted this idea, although her intense incestuous phantasies about her relationship with her father, and her experiences of degrading and shaming intrusive physical procedures, confused her, with consequent masculine identifications that were linked with power and violence. Yet this could be worked on, as long as we held on to a hope that she could change. In the end I thought something was being played out in Penny's enactments that had to be felt and experienced by me and others before she could bear to re-experience it herself and begin the task of trying to hold on to and contain it mentally and emotionally herself. At one level what was missing related to her difficulty of taking something in, retaining it and holding on to it. At another level it was simple: what was missing was her mother—shown repeatedly in her mistrust of femininity, of productiveness, and of her growing talents. In treatment her feelings about her femininity were slowly changing, in particular in her psychotherapy with her female psychotherapist working through a transference about a "useless mother". But as Penny worked on this she increasingly experienced what lay beneath, her deep despair and shame.

A turning point in getting in touch with this despair and shame was her re-experiencing, and living through quite traumatically, two events, she had until now kept secret, from the time when she was at her lowest on the streets. The first was when she beat up another girl, a stranger, for no reason, in the toilet in a night-club; the second was when she was gang raped by a group of boys. Painfully she put together what had happened to her and what she did to others, and herself, in these events and at other times. She needed to be in touch with, and own, her aggression and guilt, and to accept an understanding of how this contributed to her chaotic and destructive behaviour. There ensued a period of intense crisis, in which she thought she might end her life by acting on impulse, but she came through as she faced her despair and the ill effects of her destructiveness. She had now begun to take in a real belief in her own value, and in the future growth of her talents. Her normal adolescent self, her humour and playfulness, were strengthened, and she was now much better able to hold within herself her own anxious expectancy about the future. An engaging, though at times somewhat overbearing, ordinary adolescent side now became more dominant. Penny was for the first time actively and consistently pursuing a course in the performing arts, using her capacity for drama to good effect. With a lessening of her negative projective identification, something less intense and destructive could now come through. Shortly before leaving treatment she boasted half playfully, half anxiously, "You should get my autograph now, while you can, before I become famous!"

Penny's case illustrates the operation of both negative and positive projective identification during adolescence, and the use of excessive projective identification, seriously confusing internal and external reality, when she was highly disturbed and deeply antisocial. It also highlights the need for those attempting to contain her to be able to receive and deal with negative projective identification, through understanding and by setting adequate boundaries, and to differentiate it from positive projective identification, allowing ordinary adolescent development to continue.

My final case example is Anne, who suffered from self-harming attacks on her body and psychotic distortions in her mental states. when her projections could not be adequately received.

Anne, aged 17, had been out of school since the age of 10. She had received no subsequent schooling, and suffered chronic social and personal isolation. She had been incapable of any sustained social contact or commitment outside the family, including with groups of peers, apart from a few hours of home tuition each week. From the age of 14 and puberty, Anne was partly anorexic, severely self-harming (through disfiguring burns on her arms and legs, and cuts to her face), and a substantial suicide risk.

Anne had attended a younger-age adolescent unit for nearly two years. Subsequently she had one daily activity and her lifeline—three weekly private psychotherapy sessions for two years. She was rude and contemptuous to her analyst, but nevertheless made some progress. Anne had been a bright and happy child until her parents' acrimonious divorce when she was five. She developed an omnipotent need to take responsibility, and progressively felt her needs neglected. For two years in early adolescence, there were a number of psychotic symptoms, including a psychotic fear of holding a pen, which meant she could do no schoolwork for a long period. Although these symptoms subsided, she did not change, and remained socially isolated.

Anne also continued periodically and secretly to harm herself. She was prone to idealized love phantasies about older men, and was controlling in a regressed way, typified by her insistence that people including (even especially) professionals use a babyish form of her name. Many complied. The psychotic symptoms were not always or easily apparent, but real underlying change, for her to be able to take on an ordinary life, had also not occurred.

Her first month in the inpatient adolescent unit (cf. Flynn & Day, 2000–2001) at the hospital was an ordeal for her, which she made herself get through, sticking it out. Anne slowly began to manage the challenge of social relationships, but only as long as she kept herself emotionally distant. She and staff struggled with this, in work groups, activities and within the twice-weekly adolescent therapy group, where her tendency to take on the role of responsibility for keeping it all going was again particularly noticeable. Her fear of putting experiences together [literally "linking" and "thinking"; cf. Bion (1959, 1962a,b)], and having her own viewpoint, for fear of going mad became apparent in her individual psychotherapy. Frequently, after gaining some understanding she would evacuate it, saying she had forgotten what happened. She could easily be forgotten by staff and some patients, and remain at an emotional distance from others.

An exception to this occurred quite atypically with one adolescent [in fact, Penny, described above], who challenged her social withdrawal as due to her personal but hidden hatred of what she located in other people. This adolescent partly bullied her, but in effect also hounded her in a most useful way into a real relationship with her, and forced her to be more connected with her real needs and angry feelings. Progressively, Anne became stronger. With a developing ego strength, she has been better able to face the more disturbing aspects of her symptoms. For several months, she seemed to have remained on the brink of moving forward to something more normal, shown by her weight remaining just below a level that allowed her to have regular periods, until nearly the end of treatment.

As she progressed, she began to attend some GCSE classes, and to take on more challenging roles inside and outside the hospital. In several family meetings, separately with both her father and her mother's side of the family, she began to express her feelings about what had happened and to understand more about her role within the family. She was temporarily less confused and isolated. Her precocious over-identification with her father and the sexual fixations on older men were still, however, more apparent to us than to her, as was the depression and incapacity to bear feelings towards her mother or even her mother's feelings.

There had been, at crucial times, particularly after the divorce, a chronic pattern of almost complete denial of emotionality within the family. A significant point of progress came when Anne allowed herself to re-experience, towards the end of treatment, a reactivation of her suicide wishes. A particularly stressful and terrifying incident occurred at home on one of the final weekends in the run up to discharge. Anne tried to jump out of a second floor window, and had to be restrained by her stepfather. What happened could then, as a result of many months of treatment and family work, be recognized by her parents, and subsequently be thought about and discussed within treatment. Anne came to see that her alarming behaviour represented her increased capacity to allow her real feelings, however disturbed, to be expressed. This allowed her to differentiate her powerful but largely hidden emotions, and to use projective identification not in a negative way, by breaking links of understanding, leading to psychotic manifestations, but more positively as a way of a communicating. In this instance, she had experienced an outburst of pathological jealousy, on a trip to a cafe with her family, about another girl they had met whom she felt that others, particularly her mother, were more interested in than her. This could be linked to her pathological jealousy of her younger sister, and be seen as part of a pattern of her intense emotions and other conflicts about her mother and father, on an infantile level and as a child after the divorce, rather than something that was simply mad.

In one meeting of the adolescents near the end of treatment, as she talked with some clarity about her feelings and wishes, and withstood some of the conflict and hostility directed at her from others within the meeting, I noticed that Anne was continuously fiddling with a pen that had her real name on it, which she normally never used. She knew I always used her proper name, Anne, much to her annoyance, and never the shortened babyish form of her name that she usually insisted on.

Something important was symbolized in this small act. With her increased capacity for social relationships, and her increased ego strength, I thought she was beginning to build a new clearer identity, less regressed and hostile, but with a sense, too, of where she stood socially. The pen, which had once been feared in a psychotic way—and which, with her other disabilities, took away her education and social life—she now could hold, as just a pen. The pen was now, since she had a greater capacity to contain her emotions and experiences, more like, in Winnicott's (1971) terms, a transitional object, and Anne was learning that she could leave behind her some of her infantile identifications, and begin to cope and manage within a group of adolescents and be able to contain herself.

References

Aichhorn, A. (1931). *Wayward Youth* (English trans.). New York: Viking and London: Putnam.

Bion, W. (1957). Differentiation of the psychotic from the non-psychotic personalities. *International Journal of Psycho-analysis, 38.*

Bion, W. (1959). Attacks on linking. *International Journal of Psychoanalysis, 40.* [Reprinted in *Second Thoughts*, Karnac, 1967.]

Bion, W. (1962a). A theory of thinking. *International Journal of Psychoanalysis, 43.* [Reprinted in *Second Thoughts*, Karnac, 1967.]

Bion, W. (1962b). *Learning From Experience.* London: Kamac.

Bion, W. (1963). *Elements of Psychoanalysis*. London: Kamac.

Blos, P (1962). *On Adolescence*. New York: Free Press.

Blos, P. (1970). *The Young Adolescent*. Macmillan.

Britton, R. (1989). The missing link: parental sexuality in the Oedipus complex. In: *The Oedipus Complex Today*. London: Karnac.

Copley, B. (1993). *The World of Adolescence*, Free Association.

Erikson, E. H. (1968). *Identity, Youth and Crisis*. Faber.

Erikson, E. H. (1977). *Childhood and Society*. Paladin.

Flynn, D (1998). Psycho-analytic aspects of in-patient treatment. *Journal of Child Psychotherapy*, 24(2).

Flynn, D. (1999). The challenges of in-patient work in a therapeutic community. In: M. Lanyado & A. Horne, (Eds.), *The Handbook of Child and Adolescent Psychotherapy* (Ch. 13). London: Routledge.

Freud, A. (1936). *The Ego and Mechanisms of Defence*, Hogarth.

Freud, A., & Day, L. (2000–2001). *Mind Body Disturbance in Child and Adolescent*. London: Karnac (in press).

Freud, S. (1893). Studies in hysteria, *S.E.*, 2: 125–134. Hogarth and The Institute of Psycho-Analysis.

Freud, S. (1905). Three essays on the theory of sexuality. *S.E.*, 7: 125–243. Hogarth and The Institute of Psycho-Analysis.

Freud, S. (1914). On narcissism. *S.E.*, 14: 73–102. Hogarth and The Institute of Psycho-Analysis,.

Freud, S. (1923). The ego and the id, *S.E.*, 19: 3–66. Hogarth and The Institute of Psycho-Analysis,

Freud, S. (1925). Wayward youth (German edn), *S.E.*, 19: 272–275. Hogarth and The Institute of Psycho-Analysis. (See Aichhorn, A. *op. cit.*)

Hinshelwood, R. D. (1991). *A Dictionary of Kleinian Thought*. Free Association.

Jones, E. (1922). Some problems of adolescence. In: *Collected Papers*, Maresfield (1948).

Jones, E. (1962). *The Life and Work of Sigmund Freud*. Hogarth.

Klein, M. (1932). The psycho-analysis of children, In: *Collected Writings*, Volume 2 (pp. 80–95). Hogarth.

Klein, M. (1946). Notes on some schizoid mechanisms. *International Journal of Psycho-analysis*, 27. [Reprinted in *Collected Writings*, Volume 3, pp. 1–24. Hogarth.]

Laufer, M., & Laufer, E. (1984). *Adolescence and Developmental Breakdown*, Yale University Press.

Meltzer, D. (1994). *Sincerity and Other Works*. London: Karnac.

Rosenfeld, H. A. (1965). *Psychotic States*, Maresfield.

Rosenfeld, H. A. (1987). *Impasse and Interpretation*, Tavistock.

Salinger, J. D. (1945–1946). *The Catcher in the Rye*. Penguin.

Steinbeck, J. (1952). *East of Eden*, Heinemann.

Stern, D. (1985). *The Interpersonal World of the Infant*. Basic Books.

Winnicott, D. (1963). Hospital care supplementing psychotherapy in adolescence. [Reprinted in *The Maturational Process and the Facilitating* Environment, Hogarth (1965).]

Further reading

Waddell, M. (1988). *Inside Lives*, Duckworth.

CHAPTER FIVE

Working with addicts

Luis Rodríguez de la Sierra

T he causes of drug addiction are extremely complex and varied, and defining drug dependence is not an easy task. I will therefore refer to them in this chapter but will not attempt to solve in totality the many questions that these issues immediately bring to mind. Many of the youngsters who suffer from a compulsion to use drugs do so because of a powerful psychological dependency that pushes them towards drugs in order to avoid, regulate or run away from extremely painful and distressing inner experiences. However, the powerful psychological component of drug dependency should not make us ignore the issue of ensuing physical dependency, although I will not expand on this point as it is beyond the scope of this chapter. The question of physical dependency must be borne in mind when thinking about adolescents who are so seriously addicted to a drug that their craving becomes a major priority; in other words, those youngsters who are physiologically as well as psychologically dependent on their drugs.

Problems of substance abuse can occur at any level of society and affect all socioeconomic groups. As we know only too well, it is not necessary to come from a deprived *milieu* to become the victim of drug addiction, and patients may come from broken or intact families. The individual exists in a family and families exist in society. It is the interaction of the cultural, environmental and constitutional elements with the conscious and unconscious forces operating within the addict (or, in other words, the interaction of his or her inner and external worlds) that mostly contribute to the creation of this condition.

If we look at this problem from a developmental point of view, two basic periods must be considered: the first five years of life and the adolescent phase. I will refer to them only briefly. The first five years of life see the birth and formation of the central foundations of the personality—ego formation, cognitive development, object constancy, gender sense, social adaptation—and the development of creativity, moral sense, language, speech, etc. Without denying the importance of biological and constitutional factors, it is important to say that children who develop a firm sense of themselves, who are able to identify and control their emotions, who are capable of sustained thought and concentration—children who, in other words, enjoy good parenting will more frequently become stable individuals.

The second very important period of development, adolescence, is really our second chance to put right any unresolved crises from early childhood. This rather difficult phase is characterized by many and frequently conflicting issues. These include physical and endocrinological changes with their influence on the awakening of sexuality, academic demands, problems of identity, conflicts about dependency and independence, peer-group pressures and concerns about status.

Both childhood and adolescence are developmental stages in which we may observe either transient manifestations of internal stress or the signs of later pathology, but the problems that the ego has to deal with in adolescence are qualitatively different from those of childhood. They are now mostly related to the adolescents' reactions to the physical primacy of the genitals, the changing relationship to the original objects with the degree of psychic separateness from their internal primary objects, the difficult task of finding a new heterosexual love object and, finally, the complex task of integrating pre-Oedipal identifications, Oedipal identifications, as well as present internal and external expectations of conduct. If we take into account what goes on in terms of both the revival of infantile (pregenital) drive activity and of newly emerging urges and experiences, we realize that both have to be integrated into the existing system at the same time as a new equilibrium has to be created.

Adolescents find themselves in the very difficult position of having to make all these readjustments at the same time as they have to deal with the subsequent conflicts and anxieties. There must simultaneously be a loosening of the attachments to the same people at the centre of their fantasies and the subject of intense feelings of love and hatred. The earlier attachment and dependency on parents must now be renounced until the adolescents reach a point at which it is possible for them to confirm their own identity and find new love objects. These must neither be based too much on the repetition of previous early attachments nor be entirely and exaggeratedly opposed to them in hostility and rejection so as to make satisfactory adult life possible. It goes without saying that none of this can be achieved without much upheaval and experimenting. If, during childhood and latency, our main concern is with the child's ability to advance in both ego and drive development, in adolescence we are faced with the results of either successful or faulty structuralization that has to be understood in the context of the presence and primacy of genitality.

Needless to say, the family is very influential during both periods. When things go wrong, children and adolescents may be compelled to develop psychological and physical symptoms and illnesses as they attempt to look after themselves. Children who fail to develop what we might call strong internal worlds often seek solace in external consolations such as drugs, alcohol, sexual acting out and juvenile delinquency. It is external dependency that becomes, for many, the only unresolved means of belonging, and we then see completed in adolescence a process that started in childhood. We notice frequently that dependence in the young person is accompanied by a crisis. For the youth, childhood has passed but adult life in the future cannot always be seen clearly. The greater freedom and opportunities that adolescents have to follow their instinctual drives are not always accompanied by more tolerance of dependence on their parents as is the case until adulthood is reached.

To try and understand the reasons why young people abuse drugs is not, as I mentioned before, an easy task. A full metapsychological assessment of such cases would certainly throw greater light on the subject, but at the same time it is important to bear in mind the relevance, to the addict, of any changes in self-cathexis, in self-perception under the effect of the drugs. This leads to the question of what changes these youths may be trying to achieve.

The fact that drugs have different effects on different individuals is something we are aware of, and it is very difficult to differentiate between psychological and pharmacological effects. Talking about the specific effects of the drugs, Freud described this phenomenon clearly in "Civilisation and its discontents" (1930, p. 78):

> . . . in the last analysis, all suffering is nothing other than sensation . . . The crudest and also the most effective among these methods of influence is the chemical one—intoxication. I do not think that anyone completely understands its mechanism; but it is a fact that there are foreign substances which when present in blood or tissues, directly cause us pleasurable sensation; and they also alter the conditions governing our sensibility, so that we become incapable of receiving unpleasurable impulses.

The efficacy offered by intoxicating substances in the fight for happiness and to hold misery at bay is so greatly valued as a benefit that, according to Freud, individuals and peoples alike have given them an established place in the economics of their libido.

If we turn our attention to the question of trying to define addiction, it may be appropriate at this stage to think about the reasons why youngsters, and adults for that matter, use drugs. Anna Freud, in *From Normality to Pathology in Childhood* (1965), describes the overwhelming craving for sweets in children, who use the satisfaction of the craving as an antidote against anxiety, deprivation, frustration, depression, etc. She sees a child's love for sweets as a comparatively simple, straightforward expression of a component drive with its roots in unsatisfied or overstimulated desires of the oral phase, desires that have grown excessive and by virtue of quantity dominate his or her libidinal expressions. According to Anna Freud (*ibid.*, p. 11):

> . . . a true addiction in the adult sense of the term is a more complex structure in which the action of passive–feminine and self-

destructive tendencies is added to the oral wishes. For the adult addict, the craved-for substance represents not only an object or matter which is good, helpful, and is strengthening, as a sweet is for the child, but one which is simultaneously also felt to be injurious, overpowering, weakening, emasculating, castrating, as excessive alcohol or drugs actually are. It is the blending of the two opposing drives, of the desire for strength and weakness, activity and passivity, masculinity and femininity, which ties the adult addict to the object of his habit in a manner which has no parallel with what happens in the more benign and positively directed craving of the child.

Sigmund Freud discovered the most important link underlying drug dependence. In "Three essays on the theory of sexuality" (1905), he linked oral eroticism in men with their desire to smoke and drink. His discovery led to many subsequent psychoanalytical investigations that showed how severe drug abuse is associated not only with oral fixation, but also with disturbance in the other developmental stages and a variety of conditions, notably homosexuality and manic-depressive psychosis (Abraham, 1926; Glover, 1932).

Many adolescents use drugs for thrills, to obtain sexual gratification, and for them it is the "buzz" that really matters. They may or may not become addicted to the substance they abuse. Others take drugs for the feeling of *nirvana* they provide, to ease the despair and misery they experience. These are some of the heroin users, who, under the influence of the drug, no longer care. This was the case for the young woman artist I refer to later. Some adolescents use drugs in order to increase their self-esteem. Those who have a defect in reality testing or whose egos are weak are indifferent to the dangers of the drugs, which are outweighed by their effect on self-esteem. Other youngsters attempt to win the esteem of their peers who use drugs by following their example.

Alan, a 19-year-old heroin addict, the only child of an apparently normal family, good-looking, intelligent and a good athlete. concealed a violent nature under a pleasant and polite facade. Previous to his drug taking he had a history of outbursts of violence at school, manifested through bullying other children and occasionally gang fights and vandalism. He hated his violence and immediately conveyed to me that heroin made him feel much more peaceful, more at ease with himself, less aggressive and violent.

Let us now return to the question of trying to define drug addiction. I would like to begin by saying that I do not see these symptoms as purely neurotic or psychotic, since while it is true that the addict is more disturbed than the neurotic, it is also true that he (or she) is ostensibly less so than the psychotic.

I would like at this stage to try and clarify one common mistake and misunderstanding that tends to classify the psychopath and the addict as one and the same. While it is true that addicts may have their fair share of trouble with the law and become involved in delinquent and criminal acts, they are not to be confused with the psychopath, with whom they, by definition, cannot be classed. The psychopath experiences no internal conflict and cannot create any. Instead he establishes a conflict with the outside world and in so doing uses alloplastic methods (adaptive responses that alter the environment). The addict does experience an internal conflict and tries to resolve it by a change of endopsychic functioning, which makes his condition autoplastic (adaptive responses that alter the self). This difference is important to the proper comprehension and management of the two conditions, which I will try to illustrate with the following vignettes.

John, a 15-year-old youth, the son of divorced parents, had felt abandoned and rejected by his father, whom he had not seen since the age of 10. Undermined by his mother—who constantly criticized him and who found it difficult to tolerate his presence because he reminded her of her ex-husband—John had very poor self-esteem and had failed disastrously in his studies in spite of being highly intelligent. At school he started mixing with a "bad crowd" and began experimenting with drugs, first with hashish and afterwards with amphetamines, to which he became addicted, after experiencing, for the first time in his life, positive feelings of self-esteem. He felt that "speed" gave him a stronger, more powerful personality, which, he thought, helped him to obtain his friends' admiration. In the course of treatment he was able to acknowledge his "feelings of inferiority" and how he took drugs in order to improve himself and feel "more normal".

Linda was a 19-year-old girl who had been sent to a detention centre with a long history of antisocial activities, which included shoplifting, handling stolen goods and vandalism. She found herself a patient in an adolescent unit as a result of a probation order. She experienced no remorse over her delinquent activities and was convinced she had been caught only as a result of not being "clever enough". The family history revealed an early life of emotional deprivation and a sado-masochistic relationship with a mother, who had not helped her to master her environment, leaving her with the conviction that she could only conquer the environment by altering it if she had "special powers". Magical thinking permeated her mental life and she only responded to treatment when she felt that she was in the presence of a more powerful and clever therapist whose "magic" she could steal. [The implications of the treatment of this kind of patient have been dealt with by others (A. Aichhorn, K. Eissler, W. Hoffer).]

The unconscious conflicts of the addict arise at developmental levels that are not as early as those involved in psychoses and not as late as those of psychoneuroses. Glover (1932) thought of them as essentially transitional states: more difficult to treat than neurotics, yet clearly not psychotic or even borderline psychotic. On the other hand, most people with experience in this field have observed, in certain patients, that an addiction may preserve its victim from becoming psychotic, the role of the addiction being in their case a defensive one against psychosis.

As far as the psychopathology of the addict is concerned, the consensus on the understanding of the addictive personality classifies them under three predominant aspects: depression, paranoia and perversion, often unconscious homosexuality and sado-masochism. We often come across these combined in different proportions. To complete the picture, one should also mention other factors such as narcissism, orality, and self-destructive and destructive impulses. When considering the paranoid type, one has to be aware of how it differs from paranoid states. In these the patient is threatened by external enemies towards which he directs aggression, whereas the addict uses his drug to destroy an internal enemy. The paranoid delusion in the addict is replaced by a compulsive action, and it is this compulsion that underlines the neurotic elements in that action. It must also be mentioned here that the effects of the drugs themselves can sometimes function as conversion hysteria or as induced psychotic states divorced from reality.

According to Glover (1932), the primitive fantasies involved are of a complex nature. However, we can often see the symbolic dramatization of love and hate relationships with the parents. Pregenital fixation points are reactivated with great sadism, the intensity of which tells us how malignant the addiction is. The drug becomes an external object endowed with the loving and hateful characteristics of one or other parent. But however harmful the drug may be felt to be, it has a necessary function, since the addict feels there is something bad inside him (anxiety, guilt, perversion, psychosis, etc.), and uses the drug as if it were a medicine to anaesthetize or destroy the badness, to "cure" himself. Drug abusers are "self-medicators" who desperately and vainly try to deal with powerful, intense and disturbing inner experiences that threaten to overcome them. Unfortunately, the addict himself is, in one way or another, in danger of being destroyed.

One often observes that the young addict craves to be united with the ideal object, and one can say that when the addict develops an intense positive transference reaction when meeting an analyst, it is frequently linked with the unconscious fantasy that this ideal object has finally been found. Sadly, the conflict experienced by addicts is that, at one and the same time, they dread that union with the object and feel persecuted by it. They then become addicted to acting out the drama of fantasy introjection and separation from the drug, which is at one and the same time the analyst.

It has been said that the mildest forms of addiction are largely reinforcements of unconscious homosexuality. This does not mean they are easy to treat, particularly in adolescence for obvious reasons, and it has deeper implications in the case of the "needle" addict. The boy in conflict about his sexual identity may be unable to make a fundamental choice between the female within and the female without. The posture he adopts is overtly heterosexual, but his behaviour with drugs seem to negate this. The self-injection and the feeling of well-being that it engenders seem to symbolize and display the unconscious choice, which, however, remains unacceptable. For the girl, the problem has a similar obverse meaning and the drug abuse has the same quality as the unrestrained promiscuity that often accompanies it. Her relation to drugs progressively replaces object relations until they virtually take over.

Masturbation and sexual intercourse are often displaced by the intravenous injection of drugs.

The role of drugs in adolescence has, from a developmental point of view, many different and interesting implications. Socio-logical factors, trends, peer-group influence, etc., must be taken into account as well as psychodynamic factors when assessing psycho-pathology, for drug taking may be part of the normal adolescent's need to experiment, test or simply rebel against given adult values. This alone would, of course, be a very simplistic explanation. The use of drugs in adolescence is closely connected with failed attempts to deal with intense aggressive and sexual feelings, which the adolescent then tries to relieve by turning to pills or injections that bring deceptive tranquillity to his or her troubled mind. The analysis of many of these youngsters reveals a sado-masochistic relationship between them and their internalized objects, with its accompanying persecutory anxieties. Glover (1932) describes the symbolic dramatization of the love and hate relationship with the parents, namely a disturbed relationship between infant and mother, towards whom the adolescent remains highly ambivalent. If, to all this, we add the depression that we so very often find in adolescence, we can begin to understand the psychodynamic mean-ing of drug addiction in the young person.

Of even greater severity is the case of the confirmed addict char-acterized by a depressive organization, which, when combined with self-destructive and destructive factors, makes for an uncer-tain and poor prognosis. In this connection, I am reminded of a gifted, talented artist, a young woman in her late teens, with a long history of heroin addiction, depression and homosexual affairs. To her the needle, the syringe and the act of getting a "fix" were as important as the drug itself. She often told me that playing with the injected liquid and her blood, pushing it backwards and forwards, gave her enormous pleasure: "It is like delaying an orgasm, the more I stop it, the more I enjoy it in the end."

In common with many addicts she had appallingly low self-esteem, which convinced her from the start that, in spite of her many attempts to seduce me, I couldn't possibly even begin to like her. She constantly submitted me to innumerable tests, with the only aim seeming to be to prove her conviction that I disliked her intensely. All these "tests" contained strong self-destructive and destructive elements, which often threatened the viability of the analysis, as when she presented me with a small suitcase (that I initially interpreted wrongly as her desire to move in with me and stay near me) that turned out to be full of heroin and that would have put her at risk of being stopped by the police if she had taken it away with her. I would have found myself in a similarly difficult situation had she left it with me and I had been found in possession of it on my way home from my consulting room.

I said to her that she found herself trapped between the wish to destroy herself, and thus put an end to everything she disliked about herself, and her need to perpetrate an envious attack against me by putting me in an impossible situation. This brought back painful childhood memories. She spoke of her mother, a prostitute, who constantly brought different men to the house—men who treated her in such a way that she felt dirty and bad. She remembered her shame and her intense rage against her mother, whose death she often desired. I added that I thought she had identified with the denigrated and hated mother, whom she tried to destroy every time she attacked herself. In the transference, I was both the hated mother and the normal, sane object whom she envied intently and wished to destroy.

After this she decided the best way to solve the problem was to flush the heroin down the lavatory, insisting that I should examine the suitcase afterwards to make sure that she had disposed of everything inside it. I said it was easier to flush the heroin down the toilet than to dispose of all the badness inside her, to get rid of all the rage that she felt unable to contain. In spite of these many difficulties, a certain improvement was obtained. The patient's lover, mistaking this for a definite cure and disobeying my advice not to do so, succeeded in persuading the young woman to stop analysis and move to another country. I was not to hear about the outcome until nearly three years later. The young woman had apparently returned to the city where her mother lived. [Their relationship had continued to be rather tempestuous.] One evening my ex-patient invited her mother to the theatre. After seeing the play, before they went on to a restaurant, the young woman decided to go back to her flat to change her dress. Once there she went into a rage, insulted her mother and blamed her for all her problems. She suddenly jumped out of a window, killing herself instantly.

As the analysis of this young woman lasted only seven months, my thoughts about her basic aggressive cathexis of the self can only be speculative. Moral masochism, guilt and the need for punishment were powerful factors in the various ways in which she attacked herself. She attacked her body as a source of unwanted instinctual urges but it was also clear that the use of drugs, and the self-destructive acts that culminated with her suicide, represented a massive punitive attack on the object. The case sadly illustrates the multiple meanings that attacks on the self may have for the same patient.

Perhaps this is the moment to mention an important character trait of the addict: the highly masochistic way of relating to his or her external world, and how some of the therapeutic interventions that are offered to addicts at times exploit these masochistic tendencies. This is the case in many rehabilitation centres, where an important part of the treatment consists of a continuous battering of the patient's self-esteem with the idea that once they have been reduced to nothing they can then be "rebuilt" in a more positive way.

Rosenfeld (1960; 1964) presents a Kleinian view of addiction and thus sees it clinically as closely related, although not identical, to the manic-depressive illnesses, even where underlying paranoid feelings are masked by the manic phase. According to Rosenfeld, the addict in analysis presents a picture very similar to that of the manic depressive, and if he or she continues to take drugs during treatment, does so in order to create a state of artificial mania every time they feel threatened by depressive or paranoid anxieties. The pharmacotoxic effect of the drug is thus used to reinforce the addict's omnipotence and the mechanisms of denial and splitting. The drug reinforces the power of instinct as well as the defences against it, increases feelings of aggressive triumph, and denies any paranoid feelings in a manic revenge on supposed persecutors, thus making analysis impossible. Rosenfeld believes that a central factor in the relationship between addiction and depression is an identification with an ill or dead object. The drug is said to stand for such an object, which is then incorporated.

In my opinion, this is only true in a small number of cases. I also disagree with the idea that depressive affect and its relief can always be equated with manic-depressive states. I find some of

Rosenfeld's other ideas more useful in understanding the psychopathology of the delinquent who abuses drugs. In these cases one can see how the drug increases the delinquent's feelings of omnipotence and the magical thinking in a way that could be understood as a manic defensive mechanism.

I should like to end the subject of psychopathology by quoting Glover (1932), whose viewpoints (pp. 298–328) I find closer to my own frame of reference:

> The drug is a substance with sadistic [injurious] properties which can exist both in the outer world and in the body, but it exercises its sadistic attributes only when incorporated, it is this situation which represents a transition between, on the one hand, the menacing externalized sadism of a paranoid system, or the actual internalized sadism of a melancholic system and on the other hand, the less threatening condition that is represented by the ambivalence of the obsessional neurotic, or the hysteric to his instinctual objects.

The addiction represents, according to Glover, a strange mixture of psychic danger and reassurance. A more detailed account of Glover's views on the subject of drug addiction can be found in contributions from other authors (Limentani, 1986; Rosenfeld, 1964; Yorke, 1970). Glover repeatedly demonstrates that psychoanalysis is nothing if not a developmental psychology, and he also emphasizes the role of aggression and sadism.

The type of drug used by the person will influence our clinical judgement, since smoking cannabis cannot be equated with injecting heroin. The choice of a specific drug derives from the interaction between the psychodynamic meaning and the pharmacogenetic effect of the drug on the one hand, and the particular conflicts in a person's psychic structure throughout their development on the other. The choice of drug is certainly not as indiscriminate or capricious as it may appear from superficial observation. The anxious youth may use any drug while the young psychopath will generally take drugs that accelerate mental processes. On the other hand, the continuous use of opiates may suggest a psychotic or borderline disturbance with an important depressive element. Something similar may be said about the persistent use of alcohol, although here again it is important to remember environmental influences in certain cultures.

Changes in drug preference may also indicate internal psycho-dynamic changes. As mentioned earlier, it is extremely difficult, if not impossible, to distinguish between symptoms resulting from pharmacotoxic effects and those caused by underlying psycho-pathology. The conscious and unconscious psychological changes of adolescence, which are in a process of evolution, are further obscured by exposure to pharmacotoxic influences. Fears and anxieties accompany adolescents' curiosity about the functions of their bodies and minds; aggression and energy also become confused, and adolescents easily adopt the solution of mitigating their confusion with a "downer" rather than trying to deal with it. When initial experiments to dispose of sexual feelings through casual contacts fail, the adolescent is easily tempted to get rid of the resulting desolation, despair and emptiness by means of the instan-taneous, though temporary, relief offered by drugs.

Psychotic anxiety brought out by hallucinogenic substances such as LSD can be very frightening to the young person, who then turns to another drug to dispel the previously drug-induced distur-bance. As a result, the youngster may find solace in tranquillizers, cannabis or amphetamines. The escalation to hard drugs creates a vicious circle in which the adolescent is trapped as he or she strug-gles to keep at bay the menace of disintegration.

At the centre of the adolescent's turmoil is the revival of bisex-ual conflicts, which the young person often tries to solve through promiscuity or complete withdrawal. When these attempts fail, they may look for others in similar circumstances in the hope that sharing their problem might improve their experience. In such cases, drug abuse is the common link that constitutes the only possible elective and shared experience.

However, it is important to bear in mind that the highly ambiva-lent attitude of the addict towards the drug, first seen as a remedy and later seen as an enemy, as a persecutor to get rid of, is recreated in the transference, where the analyst becomes identified with the drug. This frequently takes place unconsciously in the mind of the patient, who has to miss sessions in order to put a distance between himself and the analyst by whom he feels persecuted and threat-ened. To interpret missed sessions as an attack against the analyst is a mistake and loses sight of the addict's need to defend himself against the imaginary attack of the analyst. Thus:

> Kevin, an intelligent and sensitive 16-year-old heroin addict, would report, after missed sessions, dreams of being persecuted by vampires who wanted to destroy him and suck his blood.

The understanding of this phenomenon and the way in which the analyst deals with it would greatly influence the possible outcome of these analyses.

It is a fact that the number of confirmed addicts asking for psychoanalytic treatment is small; their impatience and tension intolerance predispose them against the slowness of analysis. The number of analysts and psychotherapists who will accept them is even smaller and the number of addicts who complete their treatment smaller still. As in many other areas of psychopathology, there is no psychoanalytic consensus on the treatment and management of these patients. Opinions vary from those who consider these patients absolutely unsuitable for psychoanalysis to those who feel no need for any modifications whatsoever of the usual psychoanalytical approach.

I personally feel that I must respond to the addict who seeks help, but I also like to give careful thought to what sort of help I can offer. This may involve a tricky and long period of assessment, in which I must be aware of the possible complications of an incipient transference that must be dealt with, even if a patient is to be referred to somebody else. I believe that some addicts can be treated psychoanalytically, but careful consideration of the patient's individual psychopathology must be accompanied by an even more meticulous evaluation of his personal external circumstances and his environment in general (including contact with other agencies, relatives, etc.). Special consideration must be given to facts such as the severity, frequency and quality of the addiction, and whether the patient has succeeded in abandoning it before or not. If I feel that the addiction is such that to start treatment in such a state would endanger the analysis, I suggest that the addict be admitted to an institution and that detoxification be carried out by a colleague with whom I could work closely in the future if appropriate. If I decide to start treatment outside the clinic or hospital, I make sure that the adolescent's living conditions are safe, and I make a point of establishing a link or collaboration with someone living with the addict and prepared to take on the parental guiding role without which one finds it difficult to ensure the survival of the treatment or indeed of the patient. Close collaboration with other doctors involved, probation officers, social workers, hostels, etc., is to me a *sine qua non* in these cases.

I also think that, in addition to an accurate understanding of the addictive psychopathology and a great deal of empathy on the side of the analyst, one must be prepared to adopt the role of the indestructible object if one is to meet the great challenge that addicts present. By the same token, however, we must also be prepared to let the young person go when the time has come. Alan, the 19-year-old heroin addict mentioned earlier, was in analysis with me for four years. After an initial period during which I felt he was trying to frighten me with accounts of indiscriminate and dangerous drug taking, he seemed to feel reassured by my apparent lack of response. As the working alliance developed, he spoke of the deterioration of all his relationships, starting with his parents, who, unable to tolerate the stress to which he submitted them, had ended up asking him to leave home. The analysis of some of the developmental contributions to his self-destructiveness was made possible by his making me into a stronger, saner and safer object than his parents.

However, this improvement did not last long and Alan went out of his way to make analysis extremely difficult. He would either attack me, saying that my interpretations were stupid and banal, or he would miss sessions constantly. One day he came to see me after a whole week in which he had not turned up and had not even telephoned me to cancel. He had not expected to find me in my consulting room and expressed surprise at my persistence when I told him that I would always be there for his sessions, irrespective of whether he attended or not. After that session, he started to show some improvement in that he was able to reduce the amount of heroin he was injecting, and he started to attend more regularly. He was then able to see that his struggle to fight off the treatment was equivalent to his attempts to fight his drug dependence. He eventually left at the end of four years of analysis, having abandoned his heroin habit and been accepted to university. He still keeps in touch with me and I have seen him once or twice a year during the last three years. It was clear to me that in order to gain his trust and have any hopes of succeeding with him, I could not accept his destructive rejection of me and of analysis. It was also obvious that I needed to help him to separate from me and let him take on the responsibility for himself in getting accepted to university.

At this point it seems appropriate to discuss the aims and expectations of treatment of these patients. My main interest is not so much in systematically making the unconscious conscious, although I think one must deal with the emerging material via interpretative work, but only when the addict himself starts the process. The main emphasis of the analysis at that stage is to increase ego strength to the level of signal anxiety and toleration of depression. The initial aim would be to facilitate *ad maximum* the transference of addiction from the drug to the therapist, accepting from the beginning the implications of handling this sort of transference.

I do not remember ever having felt too ambitious with these patients, as I do not think one often achieves an internal psychic change of great magnitude. Even in cases where the addiction appears to have been "cured", these patients remain rather fragile and very much in need of care and support. Some of them may become patients "for life" and we must not be fooled by "pseudo" cures, for one can see they are not connected to stable, well-consolidated psychic changes but are based on identifications and introjections of an incomplete and shaky nature. On the other hand, one can often alleviate what would otherwise be a very painful and isolated existence. The main problem remains that improvement in the life of some addicts is often more superficial than in other patients and closely related to being able to preserve the good relationship to the object-analyst, even after treatment has, in theory, ended. This requires special skill on the analyst's part, and a capacity to understand and tolerate the great needs and demands of the addict.

I often think of the analysis of these patients as being divided (as in the case of some delinquents) into two phases, of which the first is a preparatory or preliminary stage. There are several factors that, I feel, must be introduced during the psychoanalytical treatment of the addict and some of them bear great resemblance to those used with delinquents, although they are present for different reasons. In her touching account of the analysis of a female addict, Julia Mannheim (1955) illustrates this point:

Many analysts agree that in the treatment of borderline cases, severely traumatized at all stages, some modifications, without impairing the neutral reserve of the analyst, are found to be necessary. Their panic stricken anxiety, deriving in part from lack of parental support, must come to a first abatement. Unless they can rely on the analyst in the role of the "ordinary, devoted mother", they behave like traumatized pre-oedipal infants and their anxiety excess does not permit them to gain insight.

During the first, preparatory phase of the analysis of these patients (indispensable for the transference of addiction), one has the double role of discovering the nature of the patient's every disturbance and of helping him to deal with affects, often by explanations and instructions. A great deal of activity and intervention in the patient's life may be necessary to reduce the level of painful affects to the point where the patient can tolerate them without drugs. Thus, some modifications in the patient's work, social or love relations may be suggested or even instituted by the therapist. Communication with relatives has to be allowed, as they must feel free to inform us of relapses or acute emergencies. The introduction of these factors may force the analyst so far into a parental role that the analysis of the transference at a later stage, the phase of analysis proper, may not always be possible. In such cases a gradual change of analyst is indicated after careful preparation and working through (with the original analyst) of the patient's reaction to the loss and rejection.

The first phase, although supportive and didactic in nature, will fail if the analyst does not interpret and does not deal with aggressive impulses that have broken through into the preconscious part of the ego, especially those that have been acted out. If one fails to deal with them, the young addict misses out on the chance to attempt conscious mastery of his or her impulses, aggression in particular. It reinforces or creates the rather frightening fantasy that the analyst is afraid of the addict's aggression and is willing to enter a collusion of silence about it. Once the phase of analysis proper has started, the final aim of analysis would have to be essentially to help the youngster to understand that ambivalence and destructiveness, the core of drug and alcohol dependence, can be contained and tolerated.

Julia Mannheim (*ibid.*) tells us that these patients' surplus of narcissism calls for postponement in dealing with the negative transference and that as many total interpretations as possible should be given, using present-day, childhood and transference material. She also quotes Greenacre (1952), who suggests that the larger outlines of behaviour tendency should never be omitted as a framework for interpretation of the finer details. Greenacre also agrees with the provision of some extra-analytic security when necessary.

In my own opinion, it is not unusual for the therapist to feel that he is engaged in child therapy and not in the treatment of an adolescent. The therapist must be prepared for an even greater degree of involvement and commitment in taking on one of these patients than is the case with others. One should be prepared for telephone calls at any time of day or night, frequent crises, visits to the patient's home, accompanying these patients to court, etc. I am fully aware of the criticism and objections that this approach will find among some colleagues.

The problems of counter-transference are very difficult, especially because of the aggression they involve. Because patients are so demanding and express insatiable and endless oral fantasies, one has to deal with fears of being devoured or destroyed, and one often becomes concerned with giving too much or too little to them. The more inexperienced or the narcissistic therapist may fall into the trap of colluding with the extreme idealization of him and may actually believe himself to be some sort of special saviour. Doctors conducting detoxification programmes and working with counter-transference problems may re-enact the behaviour of the patient's mother by not tending to his specific needs, but rejecting him angrily, ignoring him or giving him unnecessarily heavy doses of sedative medication. This may also be acted out in therapy, in the giving of unnecessary support or in insisting on the total discontinuation of the use of the drug. which is experienced by the patient as an enormously sadistic attack on the part of the therapist, at the same time as it represents an unrealistic expectation on the therapist's part. The same can be said about the tendency, among some workers in the field of drug addiction, suddenly to make the drug appear as poisonous through their, at the least thoughtless, remarks. It seems as though they fear that mentioning the drug in any other context might unnecessarily reactivate the patient's conflicts and fears on the cannibalistic level of his oral fantasies.

I would imagine that a personal understanding and handling of counter-transference problems is absolutely necessary, since such problems could prevent the psychoanalyst from recognizing the addict's specific needs and conflicts and from supplying the explanations that may increase the ego strength so as to enable it to deal with the painful affects in their regressed form.

To illustrate some of the difficulties encountered in the treatment of these patients, I would like to quote a vignette from the treatment of a 24-year-old addict, referred to me because of a long-term heroin addiction and a history of emotional and parental deprivation from a very early age.

Pierre was the only child of foreign parents who had died when he was very young. He had been brought up by a distant relative up to the age of 15, when they fell out and Pierre started living with girl-friends, who were clearly mother substitutes. When we first met I became immediately aware that he looked like, and gave the impression of being, a much younger boy, forever stuck in perpetual adolescence. He told me that his father had been a doctor and that perhaps it made sense that he should seek help from another doctor. I noticed that he was good-looking, intelligent and very articulate. It soon transpired in the analysis that he also had very poor self-esteem and saw himself as useless, stupid, ugly and "good-for-nothing". Before he took drugs, I learnt, he used to be extremely shy and completely unable to make any use of aggressive energy.

Shortly after his first intravenous injection of heroin he felt more self-confident and more able to do useful things. He felt more attractive, and soon became addicted to the feeling of increased self-esteem and well-being. Shortly before his first analytic holiday, this patient had become rather obsessed with the idea of being admitted to a detoxification centre, although he was not at the time heavily involved with drugs as during the course of analysis he had been able to reduce considerably the amount of heroin he took. For reasons that I cannot explain without betraying confidentiality. I had thought it necessary to let him know of my whereabouts during the holiday and he had insightfully admitted to fantasies of both being admitted to the drug addiction clinic where I worked at the time and/or going to spend his holiday near me. We were both aware that these fantasies were a response to the anxiety he was feeling as a result of the impending break.

On a Thursday afternoon Pierre arrived 40 minutes late and as he lay down on the couch I noticed he was sleepy and his speech was slurred. I immediately challenged him and asked him what he had taken and, after a not very convincing initial denial, he said he had taken "just a little bit of coke". I refused to believe him and asked him to stand up in order to look at his pupils, which he refused to do. I had by then decided to prolong the session as I was anxious and worried about a situation that had never before taken place during our work together. When the time of finishing the session arrived, I felt no clearer as to what had happened.

As Pierre was leaving he said that he knew I had always been interested in his poetry and he wanted to leave me a tape which contained not his poems but those of someone who wrote in a very similar style to his. I accepted the tape and as soon as my patient left, I experienced an urgent impulse to listen to it as I thought he was both very anxious and angry about my holiday and I feared what he might do. The poem on the tape made references to treacherous foreigners who deserved nothing but death and who had to be abandoned before they could become too dangerous. It was obvious that this was a reference both to his parents, by whom he felt abandoned when they died, and to me, as I was going to leave him to go on holiday. I immediately decided my patient was in very serious danger and, preferring to take the risk of being an alarmist, I telephoned him. There was no reply. I then remembered that the social worker involved in the case lived near him and I rang her up and asked her to knock at the door and to call me back immediately if she got no reply. I telephoned for an ambulance. It transpired that my patient had taken an overdose of heroin and was taken immediately to casualty where, by that night, he was out of danger as the overdose had not been massive. He telephoned me the following day saying that he was going to discharge himself and asking me to see him on Saturday, which I did. During that session he suddenly remembered something that he said he had never thought about since he was a child. His father apparently used often to go abroad for lectures and the little boy always managed to cut himself or have an accident before his father's departure to try to compel him to stay. Pierre broke down in tears and was able to talk with much feeling about the events which were a re-enactment, in the transference, of past events involving his father during his childhood.

I am aware that I have left out many important things and that the validity of the points I have referred to in this chapter can only be verified by the analysis of other similar cases. My main intention in writing this chapter has been to provoke interest and enthusiasm in those of you who may consider helping this neglected group of patients, who, although difficult, are as entitled to ask for, and obtain, help as anyone else.

References

Abraham, K. (1926). The psychological relation between sexuality and alcoholism. *International Journal of Psycho-analysis*, 7: 2–10.

Freud, A. (1965). *From Normality to Pathology in Childhood*. New York: International Universities Press.

Freud, S. (1905). Three essays on the theory of sexuality. *S.E.*, 7. Hogarth and The Institute of Psycho-Analysis.

Freud, S. (1930). Civilisation and its discontents, *S.E.*, 21. Hogarth and The Institute of Psycho-Analysis

Glover, E. (1932). On the etiology of drug addiction. *International Journal of Psycho-analysis*, 13, 298–328.

Greenacre, P. (1952). *Trauma, Growth and Personality*. New York: International Universities Press.

Limentani, A. (1986). *On the Psychodynamics of Drug Dependence* (pp. 48–65). Free Association.

Mannheim, J. (1955). Notes on a case of drug addiction. *International Journal of Psycho-analysis*, 36: 166–173.

Rosenfeld, H. (1960). On drug addiction. *International Journal of Psycho-analysis, 41*, 467–475.

Rosenfeld, H. (1964). The psychopathology of drug addiction and alcoholism: a critical review of the psychoanalytic literature. In: *Psychotic States*, [reprinted Hogarth, 1965].

Yorke, C. (1970). A critical review of some psychoanalytic literature on drug addiction. *British Journal of Medical Psychology*, 43: 141–184.

Further reading

Boyd, P. (1972). Adolescent drug abuse and addiction. *British Medical Journal, 4*, 540–543.

Fenichel, 0. (1945). Drug addiction. In: *The Psychoanalytic Theory of the Neurosis*, pp. 377–379. New York: Norton.

Heimann, P. (1949–1950). On counter-transference. In: *Collected Papers: About Children and Children No Longer* (New Library of Psycho-Analysis 10). London: Routledge

Heliman, I. (1964). Observations on adolescence in psychoanalytic treatment. *British Journal of Psychiatry, 110*: 406–410.

Rodriguez de la Sierra, L. (1990). 'El vampiro' in *Mitos*, Volume I, pp. 205–215. Lima (Peru): Sociedad peruana de psicoanalisis.

Sandler.J. (1976). Countertransference and role responsiveness. *International Review of Psycho-analysis, 3*, 43–47.

Appendix: agencies working with adolescents

Anna Freud Centre (020) 7794 2313

Brandon Centre (020) 7267 4792

Brent Adolescent Centre (020) 7328 0918

City Road Youth Counselling (020) 7250 1829

Croydon Youth Counselling (020) 8680 0404

Highgate Counselling Centre (020) 8883 5427

Islington Women's Counselling (020) 7281 2673

Just Ask (020) 7628 3380

Lincoln Centre (020) 7978 1545

The London Clinic of Psycho-Analysis (020) 7563 5002

Nafsiyat: The Intercultural Therapy Centre (020) 7263 4130 / 7561 1870

Off Centre (020) 8985 8566

Open Door Group (020) 8348 5947

Park Side (020) 7221 4656

The Portman Clinic (020) 7794 8262

Tavistock Clinic Y.P.C.S. (020) 7435 7111

Westminster Pastoral Foundation (020) 7937 6956

INDEX